WHAT YOU NEED TO KNOW ABOUT

LEADERSHIP

JEFF GROUT & LIZ FISHER

CAPSTONE

D0496192

This edition first published 2011
© 2011 Jeff Grout and Liz Fisher

Registered office
Capstone Publishing Ltd. (A Wiley Company), The Atrium, Southern
Gate, Chichester, West Sussex, PO19 8SQ, United Kingdom

For details of our global editorial offices, for customer services and for
information about how to apply for permission to reuse the copyright
material in this book please see our website at www.wiley.com.

```
LIBRARIES NI

C700652430

RONDO            26/05/2011

658.4092         £ 12.99

HLWDSE
```

Library of Congress Cataloguing-in-Publication Data

9780857081308 (paperback), 9780857082145 (ebook),
9780857081681 (epub), 9780857081698 (emobi)

A catalogue record for this book is available from the British Library.

Set in 10.5/13.5 New Baskerville by Toppan Best-set Premedia Limited

Printed in Great Britain by TJ International Ltd., Padstow, Cornwall

CONTENTS

INTRODUCTION

Congratulations. The fact that you have opened this book suggests that you have either been recently promoted to a leadership position, or expect to at some point in the future. Or, perhaps you are thinking of setting up your own business and want to know what to expect when you employ a team of workers. Either way, well done. You have ambition, but you are also wise enough to know that leadership is something you have to learn about, and not necessarily something that you are born knowing what to do.

People are called on to lead in all walks and at all stages of life – in sport and games when we are children, at work, in politics, and at times of crisis and uncertainty. But at no point does someone sit us down and tell us what to do, and what leadership is all about. When an eight-year-old is made captain of his football team, or a teenager is elected head boy or girl of their school, they have no real idea that they will be and are being a leader. They just do it. Some do it well, and some do it badly, and most just muddle through. And exactly the same thing applies when we get older.

Almost all of us, in our working lives, will at some stage in our career, be asked to lead someone (or, even better, a group of someones). A few will reach the very top of the business tree, and lead a large company. But the chances are that none of us will ever have had anything that could be described as formal training on how to lead. So, when we first find ourselves in a leadership situation we wonder, what am I supposed to do? How am I supposed to behave? And how on earth can I be sure that these people will do what I say?

Few of us could explain exactly what a leader is, what leadership means in an everyday context, and what works (or doesn't). Almost all of us will have had bosses ourselves, though, and the chances are that a few of them were not very good. Perhaps some of these sound familiar:

▶ The scary boss – he (or often she) is inapproachable, given to shouting and really quite intimidating. But people tend to do what they say, generally because to do otherwise would risk untold wrath.

▶ The distant boss – who sits in an office behind a closed door, sometimes in a different office. If you met them in a lift, you'd struggle to recognise them and they probably wouldn't have much of a clue about you, either.

▶ The inept but nice boss – very friendly and great in social situations, but disorganised and frustrating to be around at work.

▶ The promoted-beyond boss – great at the mechanics of what they do, but without much of a clue about people management.

▶ The watch-yourself boss – pleasant and friendly on the outside but unlikely to protect you when things get tough, or prone to taking credit for someone else's ideas or work.

Our experiences should tell us that there are many potential minefields to being a leader. It might be difficult to pin down exactly what someone is doing wrong, but few of us ever forget being led by a poor leader. But, on the other hand, we all remember and respect our good bosses – the ones who encouraged us to do our best, supported us, praised us quietly when we did well and accepted our mistakes with dignity. These are the people you want to emulate when you are a leader yourself.

This book is designed to help you become that boss. It covers all of the key issues that leaders have to face and deal with, and the key techniques that the best leaders use (and yes, they are techniques) to persuade people to follow them and to produce their best for them. The book is split into eight chapters:

1. What is Leadership?
2. Creating a Vision
3. Building a Team
4. Communication
5. Motivation and Inspiration
6. Performance Management
7. Leading Change
8. Leading in Turbulent Times

Because the business world is diverse, varied and unpredictable, and because every leader and every employee is different, we've used a lot of real-life examples from companies in range of industries, as well as the views and experiences of leaders in other disciplines, such as sport and the military, to explain some of the leadership theories we cover in the book. A leader is a leader in any field, and the best business leaders look well beyond their own horizons to learn whatever they can from others. Few people can claim to know more about leading men in stressful situations than military leaders, and they have important lessons to tell us.

Together, the material in the book should explain clearly to you how the best leaders gather talented people around them and persuade them to work to their limits in pursuit of a common goal, whatever that goal may be. And because no two organisations are the same and because life, particularly business life, is unpredictable, it will also tell you how to cope with the unexpected – and how the unexpected can, in fact, be a good thing.

There are some common features in each of these chapters, which add to the detail and point you in the direction of more information, should you want to follow anything up:

> ▶ **What it's all about** – The beginning of each chapter gives a quick summary of what you can expect.
> ▶ **Who you need to know** – A few of the important people you need to know in the field of leadership, including the best-known academics who have studied the subject, well-known writers on

leadership and some high-profile business leaders.

▶ **Who said it** – Quotes from well-known leadership figures to inspire and remind you of the key points

▶ **What you need to read** – A few suggestions for further reading and online resources on the subjects covered in each chapter, should you want to explore some more.

▶ **If you only remember one thing** – A re-run of the most important idea in each chapter.

This is not a book about how to be a particular type of leader; it is a book about how to be yourself as a good leader. The best leaders are not actors – they are essentially being themselves. What is different about them is their ability to persuade, motivate and inspire others to be their best. And this is something that can be learned. So start reading, and bring out the future leader in you.

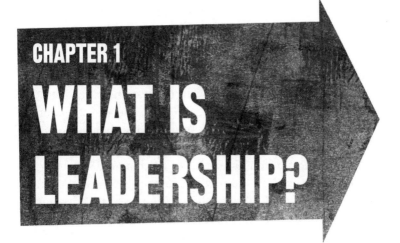

CHAPTER 1
WHAT IS LEADERSHIP?

WHAT IT'S ALL ABOUT ➡

- ▶ The distinction between leadership and management
- ▶ How the way we think about leadership has developed
- ▶ The essential leadership characteristics
- ▶ What leaders really do

The world has been fascinated by leadership for as long as man has stood upright. Rather than celebrate collaborative effort, it has long been the case that much of the credit for the success of a group (or responsibility for the failure) is laid at the feet of its leader. Successful leaders have been lauded, admired, honoured and even worshiped. Leaders who were unfortunate enough to oversee a disaster shouldered almost all of the blame. Underlying everything is a fundamental curiosity over why some people lead and others follow. The characteristics and actions of leaders throughout history have been examined for clues and many attempts – some more scientific than others – have been made to identify the qualities that make for a great leader, with little consensus. And still the debate goes on.

The business world is not unusual in attributing more credit than is perhaps strictly due in the success of a company to its leader. *Fortune* magazine, which regularly publishes its list of America's most admired companies, argues that there are many factors that, considered together, make a company admirable in the eyes of others. But if people were forced to select just one determining factor, they will inevitably say that business success is mainly down to strong leadership (by which they mean the chief executive, managing director or chairman).

Given the emphasis that the business world places on leadership as a vital element in growth and success, there is a constant search for good leaders and for future leaders. Anyone with any ambition in business hopes to be singled out as future leadership potential. If you want to get to the top, you will have to be a leader.

But what does it mean to be a leader? What do leaders really do? The truth is that most of us will be called up to perform a leadership role at some point in our lives, inside or outside work. Leadership skills are far more widely called upon in life than many realise, but few of us could clearly explain what leadership is, what it entails, and what works (or doesn't). So we tend to muddle through and do the best we can, through trial and error.

WHO SAID IT

"Leadership is the art of getting someone else to do something you want done because he wants to do it."
– Dwight D. Eisenhower

There is no shortage of literature and advice available for anyone who is aiming for a leadership role in the future. Type 'leadership' into Google, for instance, and you will get well over a million hits. Tens of thousands of books on leadership have been published, from highly technical explanations of the latest management model to autobiographies of those who have led successfully in their own chosen field. But underlying all of the technical theory and discussion are a series of skills and techniques that are common to successful leaders. Not all leaders are the same, by any means – as we will see, the trick in being a good leader is to adapt your own personality to a leadership situation – but all good leaders use similar techniques to encourage people to follow them. The good news is that leadership skills can be learned. If you know what to do, you can be a good leader.

THE DISTINCTION BETWEEN LEADERSHIP AND MANAGEMENT

Being a leader is not the same as being a manager. Some leadership theorists argue that you can be appointed a manager but you have to earn your role as leader. That's not entirely the case but it does explain why some leaders fail so spectacularly. You can be appointed a leader but you can't remain one without followers – and in the modern world, people will only fall in behind you if they think you are worth following.

The distinction between management and leadership is often used to illustrate what it is that makes for a successful leader, as well as what it is that leaders really do. The debate was kicked off in 1977 when an article, 'Managers and Leaders: Are They Different?' by Abraham Zaleznik, appeared in the *Harvard Business Review*. In the article, which has become one of the most famous in leadership studies, Zaleznik argued that where managers look for order and control, and work to rapidly resolve any problems they face, leaders tend to tolerate chaos and lack of structure and occasionally avoid offering a solution for the sake of innovation.

Zaleznik argued that managers and leaders were fundamentally different in the way they work with others, and in their attitude towards goals. Leaders, he said, shape rather than respond to ideas and change how people think about what's desirable and possible. The goals of managers, on the other hand, arise out of necessity rather than desire. Leaders seek risk when opportunities seem to be promising, whereas managers tend to avoid risk. And while managers communicate by giving unambiguous signals and tend to be emotionally detached from their subordinates, leaders communicate directly and by appealing to human emotions. Zaleznik's article is sometimes seen as being rather hard on managers, but in fact he points out that organisations need both managers and leaders to survive.

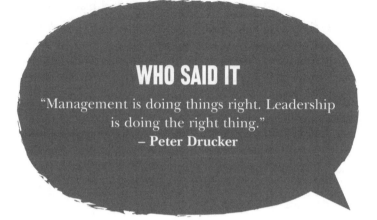

WHO SAID IT

"Management is doing things right. Leadership is doing the right thing."
– **Peter Drucker**

In business terms, management is about planning, budgeting, organising and problem-solving. Leaders may manage on a day-to-day basis but their ultimate role is far more significant. Leaders establish a direction for the group or organisation. And once they have decided on a direction they must communicate it to everyone, persuade everyone to buy into the idea and motivate them to achieve the target. Leadership and change, as we will see in Chapter 7, go hand in hand – change cannot happen without leadership.

This is, effectively, the modern view of leadership, in which the leader sets the 'dream', or direction, for the organisation and uses his or her skills in motivating and inspiring people to persuade them to perform at their best in order to achieve it. But this is a relatively new interpretation of the role of the leader – as we go back in history, the view of the leader had more in common with what Zaleznik might see as a manager. In other words, where modern leaders lead through power of persuasion and inspiration, in the past leaders have led through authority, hierarchy or sometimes fear.

A SHORT HISTORY OF LEADERSHIP

For almost as long as leaders have led, attempts have been made to understand what makes a leader, and what behaviour and characteristics differentiate leaders from followers. Early analysis of leadership, for example, can be seen in many pieces of classical literature. In *Parallel Lives*, for example, Plutarch discusses what impact the character of a man has on his destiny. Many of Shakespeare's plays stuffed full of studies of leadership: good leaders (*Henry V*), hopeless leaders (*Henry VI, Richard II*), flawed leaders (*Coriolanus*) and even potentially strong leaders who used their power to gain a position to which they had no right, and then die horribly (*Macbeth, Henry IV*).

The first works almost solely devoted to the question of leadership, though, can be traced to the mid-nineteenth century. The Scottish historian and philosopher Thomas Carlyle published two books in the 1840s, *Heroes and Hero Worship* and *The Letters and Speeches of Oliver Cromwell*, which attempted to deconstruct the qualities and characteristics of leaders throughout history. Another Victorian intellectual (and a distant relative of Charles Darwin), Sir Francis Galton, began exploring at around the same time the question of whether human ability (and leadership qualities) were genetically linked. The result of his research, *Hereditary Genius*, was published in 1869.

These early works were essentially variations of a view that had been long held – that leaders were born, and could not be made. This may have had its roots in the belief, documented time and time again in Shakespeare's works, of the 'divine right of kings' – that God decided who was to lead the country and therefore, leaders must have been chosen before their birth by the same divine hand. This view reached its peak at the turn of the twentieth century, when studies of leadership tended to concentrate on the political and social élite. Some men (inevitably they were men) were born to lead and the rest of us, well, all we could do was watch. The First World War did much to debunk this myth, as many a 'great man' proved to be less than effective as a military strategist or motivator of the troops.

This can be seen quite clearly in the way the accepted definition of leadership has changed over the years. In 1927, for instance, one definition of leadership read that it was 'the ability to impress the will of the leader on those led and to induce obedience, respect, loyalty and cooperation'. But by 1942 this definition had developed: 'Leadership is the art of influencing, as opposed to compelling, people by persuasion or example to follow a line of action'. This is result of more the sophisticated analysis of leadership theory began to emerge in the late 1920s and early 1930s, when people began to explore the specific skills displayed by leaders and the situational factors that might affect their behaviour, rather than focusing on the qualities of individual leaders.

Since then, leadership theory has developed in a series of distinct stages. That is not to say that one theory would disappear as the next one emerged – some are still argued vehemently today, while others have faded away only to reappear again a few years later in an embellished form. And the accepted view of leadership has steadily changed with each new study and leadership model so, for instance, the view in the 1960s was that leadership was 'a series of acts by persons which influence other persons in a shared direction', while by the turn of this century academics were talking about leadership as 'ultimately about creating a way for people to contribute to making something extraordinary happen'.

SOME ARE BORN 'GREAT'

Taking all the developments over the twentieth century, the way that academics and others think about leadership can be loosely sorted into several categories. The traditional and long-standing view that leaders are born and not made is known as 'Great Man' theory. While some would still argue that some people are born with a personality type that makes some sort of leadership role inevitable, the 'Great Man' theory has been comprehensively disproven and is now considered to be terminally unfashionable. 'Great Man' theory is closely connected to the 'command and control' view of leadership, which many people traditionally see as a military style of leadership (this is inaccurate, incidentally, since modern military leaders stress above all the importance of gaining the trust and respect of their men and rarely lead purely through the command structure). Command and control was particularly prevalent in the first half of the twentieth century and is still enthusiastically practiced by some leaders today (although generally not those who are considered to be good). As the name suggests, it is a leadership style that is based on authority, unquestioning acceptance of orders by the followers, and often fear.

Once the 'Great Man' view of leadership began to fall out of favour, people began to wonder if leaders all possessed some specific personality traits that set them apart from others. This view of leadership is known as trait theory, and argues that leadership is based on individual attributes. The Victorian studies of Galton and Carlyle were early versions of this approach, in their attempts to identify the behavioural characteristics and unique talents of leaders. Several studies during the 1930s and 1940s attempted to identify universal traits that were common to all leaders – suggestions put forward include decisiveness, adaptability, self-confidence, intelligence, insight and initiative – but consensus on a definitive list was never reached. As a result trait theory fell out of favour, but the term is still widely used today.

LEADERS' BEHAVIOUR

The next step in the examination of what makes a leader was to look at the behavioural characteristics of leadership. One of the early and most influential figures in this movement was an American psychologist of German descent, Kurt Lewin. Lewin developed a theory (now known as Lewin's equation, $B = f(P,E)$) that argued that behaviour is a function of the person and their environment. He applied his observations of behavioural psychology to the study of leadership and in 1939 published a paper, with his colleagues Ronald Lipitt and Ralph White, which identified three leadership styles: autocratic leadership; participative (or democratic) leadership and laissez-faire leadership. The research clarified some of the leadership theories that had been developed until that point, and would form the foundations of theoretical studies in the future.

Briefly, Lewin defined autocratic leadership (seen in the command and control approach) as one where leaders made decisions alone and demanded strict adherence to the path they set. The decision-making power is centralised, and although the leader is not necessarily hostile, he does not contribute to the work carried out by others. Praise and criticism of followers plays a significant role in authoritative leadership. A participative leadership style is one where the leader asks for input and suggestions from others, before deciding on the direction for the group. Praise or criticism is offered subjectively by the leader. Laissez-faire leadership, by contrast, allows the group to make decisions for themselves without any input from the leader unless they are specifically asked to participate, and little praise or criticism of followers is offered. Lewin's research of the three styles using a control group suggested that the democratic style was the most popular among followers.

Behavioural theory faltered as an academic pursuit when researchers found that they were unable to identify a definitive list of behaviours to define leadership. However, behavioural theory was one of the first models to suggest that leadership skills could be learned.

ADAPTABLE LEADERS

In the 1960s, emphasis shifted towards identifying the behaviour patterns of leaders that work in specific situations, which resulted in the development of the contingency view of leadership. The theory argues that there is no single style of leadership that will work in all situations, and that good leadership depends on a number of factors, including the quality of the followers. A variation of this theory is situational leadership, which argues that leaders assess their environment and the conditions of the moment before deciding on a course of action. From an academic point of view the research proved to be too complex to follow to any conclusion as it was clear that there were an infinite number of situations and environmental factors that could influence a leader's behaviour.

Transactional leadership – sometimes referred to as managerial theory – is one of a number of leadership models that has emerged in the past 30 years. Transactional theory could be characterised as the 'carrot and stick' approach to supervision and management of the team, or the straightforward exchange of work for pay and benefits. The aim is to encourage performance through a reward and punishment approach – if employees are successful at their given task they are rewarded and if they fail, they are reprimanded.

In more recent times people have begun to concentrate on a leader's ability to persuade people to follow them, rather than on their control over others' behaviour. The participative approach to leadership, for example, argues that successful leaders encourage participation from followers and actively welcome input and contributions, with the result that followers feel more involved and are more committed to successfully achieving the outcome. Many modern academics often talk about participation theory, or about transformational leadership, which concentrates on the relationship between leader and followers and argues that a successful leader has the ability to change their followers in a way that results in their being motivated to perform at a higher level than before. Transformational leaders are seen as inspirational, with excellent communication skills and great emotional intelligence.

By the 1980s, academics had begun to abandon the idea of identifying a single theory that could explain all leadership styles, and instead concentrated on researching the best and most successful companies and their leaders in an effort to identify the factors that contributed to excellence. These might include the personality and behaviour of the leader, the corporate culture and working environment and team dynamics.

WHERE WE ARE TODAY

The different and varying paths that academic research into leadership has followed over the years should be a clue that there is no simple answer to the question of what makes a great leader. The truth is that any of the approaches to leadership described here – even the largely discredited command and control approach – have their place in modern-day leadership. There are simply some occasions where the right thing to do is to give an order, and see that it is followed through.

WHO SAID IT

"When I first got into management I used to think about the right way to behave, and I think that came from a lack of self-confidence. The conclusion I've come to over the years is not that anything goes, but that there are a vast variety of effective leadership styles."
– **Martin Glenn (CEO Birds Eye Iglo)**

This is the modern-day view of leadership: the recognition that different situations call for different leadership approaches, and a good leader is adept at recognising those situations and adapting their behaviour accordingly. The leadership style for each situation should achieve the overall objective of the group, without demotivating individual members. That said, it is widely accepted now that the most successful leaders are those that inspire their followers to perform well, rather than terrify or coerce them into it. This has a lot to do with the way that our working lives and career structure has changed over the past few decades. Fifty or sixty years ago it was normal for a worker to join a company straight out of school or university and stay there until retirement. These days we are more flexible and exercise far more control over our own careers. We move from organisation to organisation, and sometimes from sector to sector. If we don't like a company or our job or our boss – and the evidence is that their immediate boss is the most common reason anyone gives for leaving a company – we find another one.

In this world where careers are seen as moveable feasts and organisational loyalty is on the wane, the argument is that people want to be led by leaders who inspire them to do the best they can. If they have a bad leader, at best they will be demotivated and at worst, will actively sabotage the endeavour.

One of the consequences of this shift over time in the view of what makes for a good leader is that the skills necessary to be successful have changed. Whereas decades ago a sense of authority was seen as the key skill, today it is emotional intelligence, or the ability to read people, to work out how to get the best out of them, and adapt your behaviour accordingly.

In 2006, Rob Goffee and Gareth Jones published a book (*Why Should Anyone Be Led By You?*) which talked of 'authentic' or 'empathetic' leadership, which neatly sums up the modern view of leadership. Goffee and Jones concentrated on leaders who excel at inspiring people, and on a leadership style that is 'antibureaucractic and charismatic'. They argue in the book that while it is not essential to have leaders in business with these qualities, it is unlikely that a company will ever achieve great results unless they have such a leader.

WHO YOU NEED TO KNOW
Rob Goffee and Gareth Jones

Goffee and Jones are leadership academics
and consultants, best known for their book
Why Should Anyone Be Led By You? Rob
Goffee is professor of organisational
behaviour at London Business School,
while Gareth Jones was director of human
resources and internal communications
at the BBC during Greg Dyke's tenure as
leader, and is now a visiting professor at
INSEAD and a fellow at London Business
School. Together, they have spent almost
30 years exploring leadership in
theory and practice.

Why Should Anyone Be Led By You? introduced
the concept of 'authentic' leadership and
quickly became an influential force in the
way leadership is viewed. In the book, Goffee
and Jones argued that the modern

world had become disenchanted with the 'able role player' or 'skilled apparatchik' in all walks of life and particularly in business and in politics. Instead, Goffee and Jones wrote that what organisations and followers need and want are real people with personalities that we all recognise, or, as they put it, 'authentic leaders who know who they are, where the organisation needs to go, and how to convince followers to help them take it there'.

Goffee and Jones argue that the best modern leaders understand this, and take active steps to 'show' themselves to their followers, flaws and all. The book uses a series of real-life examples to show that the best leaders are 'authentic chameleons' who are themselves as much as possible in their leadership role, but who adapt their personality and behaviour according to the situation in hand.

Goffee and Jones say that leadership is about results, but add that really great leadership has the potential to excite people to extraordinary levels of achievement. Their central point is that leaders at all levels make a difference to performance, but that they do so by making performance meaningful. They argue that 'authentic' leaders recognise that people want to be led by a human being; authentic leaders are purposefully human and selectively reveal their weaknesses to followers. They identify what makes them successful as a leader and play to those strengths – being themselves, but a selectively edited version. This, of course, requires a high degree of self-awareness.

Empathetic leaders concentrate on getting the best out of their followers by making an effort to know and understand them. They carefully manage their relationships with others and know when to empathise in order to encourage loyalty, and when to keep their distance, without resorting to hierarchy. In other words, they know how to inspire loyalty and respect, and sometimes even affection, while maintaining some professional distance. Their followers work hard for them because they trust them and crucially, want to impress them.

ESSENTIAL LEADERSHIP CHARACTERISTICS

So what qualities do you need to be a good leader today? Many attempts have been made to come up with a definitive inventory of characteristics that make for a good leader and if you put all of the suggestions together, the list would be endless. But there are a few core qualities that crop up time and time again, in various guises.

The first is integrity. When people talk about the integrity (or honesty or fairness or moral courage) of a leader what they mean is that followers must believe absolutely in their leader and in what they are all trying to do. Military leaders stress this above everything else, and talk about the potentially devastating impact on soldiers' morale if they are not convinced that the cause they are fighting for is right and that their leaders are fully committed to it. That said, there have clearly been a number of leaders over the years lacking in integrity whose followers, presumably, followed them through fear. Most, fortunately, have reached a sticky end.

Passion, or enthusiasm, is another basic requirement of a good leader. Leading a team or company takes a great deal of energy and a leader cannot sustain the motivational force needed to keep everyone moving in the same direction unless they have unbridled enthusiasm for what they are doing. Effective leaders are absolutely committed to their company, rather than to their pay packet.

WHO SAID IT

"Innovation distinguishes between a leader
and a follower."
– Steve Jobs (CEO Apple)

Competence is another basic necessity. It's unlikely that
a leader will ever gain the respect needed to inspire their
followers if they lack the skills that they are asking others
to excel in. Even if they are not doing themselves what
they are asking others to do for them, leaders should at
the very least be able to understand exactly what they are
asking of their people. Leaders who are excellent at the
underlying job have a head start in gaining and keeping
the respect of their followers. This is particular true of
sporting leaders, who are expected to lead by example
and from the front – there is nothing more demotivating
for a team than seeing their captain struggle to score
runs or goals.

Competence and integrity tend to build what is often
identified as a characteristic of great leaders, and that is

mutual respect. As we've seen, modern leaders no longer rule through fear or control but by taking an interest in their followers, by caring about them and what they do. It is this that wins their followers' trust and respect. Creating this atmosphere of mutual respect brings many benefits and in particular fosters an atmosphere where people are likely to tell their leader when there is a problem, which gives a leader a fighting chance, at least, of tackling it before it gets out of hand.

Leaders must also be forward-thinking. The fundamental role of a leader is to set the direction for the organisation, to select the best way forward when they might be faced with seemingly endless choices and a current environment that seems less than stable. Finding a path and sticking to it – as well as anticipating change and recognising when it is time to shift direction – is the most difficult thing a leader will do and demands a clear mind, steely resolve and a willingness to take calculated risks. Leadership researchers sometimes talk about a leader's need to harness 'creativity', and argue that successful leaders are constantly on the lookout for the next opportunity and show an unwillingness to accept the status quo.

EMOTIONAL INTELLIGENCE

In many ways modern leadership is more about emotions than it is about logic. Modern leadership depends to a large extent on the leader's ability to read people, to assess their strengths and weaknesses, to judge collective mood, and to encourage performance by fanning the enthusiasm of followers. This demands a degree of emotional intelligence (defined as the ability to recognise and manipulate or control – hopefully in a positive sense – the emotions of other people, as well as your own). Some business leaders do manage to get by without being particularly good with people, but their task is that much more difficult.

Emotional intelligence as a subject began as far back as Charles Darwin, who discussed the importance of emotional expression in human survival, but it was not directly linked to the field of leadership until the 1980s. A huge range of studies, papers and books on the subject have been produced since then, most of which discuss leadership in terms of social awareness and the ability to manage relationships, as well as self-awareness of the leader (being aware of their emotions, realising what impact they will have on others and adapting them to specific circumstances). Opinions vary widely in academia on whether emotional intelligence has any serious validity as a subject in itself, but there is little doubt that many modern leaders do have this ability to read people's emotions and actively try to harness their power.

LEARNING FROM EXPERIENCE

The best lessons in leadership come from the leader's own experiences, and from watching, encountering and reading about the experiences of others. It's pretty much impossible to become a leader without having been a follower at some point, which gives a future leader an excellent perspective of what works in terms of leadership and what does not. Leaders frequently develop leadership styles that are heavily influenced by bosses they have worked under in the past. A small number of very lucky people will find themselves mentored into a leadership position but most future leaders have learned through experience and by trial and error – hopefully other people's errors other than their own – by carefully watching what other leaders do. This is also why books by well-known business leaders, such as Jack Welch, are so popular.

WHO YOU NEED TO KNOW
Jack Welch

Jack Welch was CEO and chairman of the US giant General Electric between 1981 and 2001.

He is revered in the US as one of the most successful business leaders in recent times and as a result his books on business and leadership, most notably *Winning*, have become best-sellers.

Unlike many other leadership writers, Welch can claim undeniable evidence that his approach to leadership worked in practice – during his time as CEO, General Electric's market value increased from $12 billion to over $400 billion. Welch joined GE in 1960 and by the time he became its youngest ever chairman 21 years later, he was convinced that the organisation was bloated and overly bureaucratic. His time as CEO was characterised by cost-cutting and he is credited by some for inventing the notion of 'downsizing' in order to keep a business efficient – during his first five years as CEO, headcount at GE fell from 411,000 to just under 300,000. He demanded high performance from everyone and became notorious for firing the 10% worst-performing managers every year. In 1999 he was named 'Manager of the Century' by *Fortune* magazine. Since retiring, Welch has written a series of business and leadership books, including *Jack: Straight from the Gut.*

Remembering the effect that bosses have had on you, good and bad, is a very good guide for refining your own style of leadership. Irrespective of the pressure that you might find yourself under as a leader, it is always a good idea to stop and ask yourself from time to time: What does it feel like to be led by me?

THE CHARISMA QUESTION

The question of whether charisma (meaning the natural ability to inspire enthusiasm or affection among others through the power of personality) is a basic requirement of a leader crops up frequently. The simple answer is, no, but it certainly helps. Charisma is not a requirement but a leader that does not have it will have to work that much harder in order to win people over. Charisma is, essentially, a short-cut in the battle to encourage followers (which is why it is most frequently found in politicians).

The good news is that charisma can be approximated to a certain degree, or at least learned. Anyone who has been in the presence of a charismatic leader – and one of the best examples of recent times is the former US President Bill Clinton – will say that they have an uncanny ability to make you feel like the most important person in the room, if only for a few moments. In President

Clinton's case, the reaction is not entirely accidental. He is currently the most expensive public speaker in the world and if you can afford to book him he will include a personal reception before or after the event for up to 15 people. Before the reception he asks for a short biography of everyone who will attend and then, for an hour, he works the room. He will greet everyone with a handshake and a hand on the arm, or wrist or shoulder – everyone is different – and engage them in a conversation that, to them, is entirely personal. For those few minutes, his eyes will never waver from theirs and as anyone who has met him will tell you, it is hypnotic stuff.

Charisma often has a lot to do with theatrical behaviour – an air of confidence, strong body language, a persuasive speaking style. But above all, it is about being memorable and many a successful leader who has found to be lacking in the charisma department has made use of other tactics in order to ensure that they remain lodged in the mind. In some cases it is a quirky dress sense – think of the Apple CEO Steve Jobs, for example, and you will picture him in jeans, a black jumper and trainers. That's because he has worn a variation of that same combination for as long as he has been in the public eye. Coincidence? A lack of sartorial imagination? Or a relatively easy way of marking himself as different? Richard Branson, founder of Virgin, is instantly recognisable, mainly because he doesn't particularly resemble the traditional view of the CEO of a multinational company.

WHAT DO LEADERS ACTUALLY DO?

So, we have a rough list of characteristics that make for an effective leader, and an idea of what modern leadership requires. But what do leaders really do, from one day to the next?

The very best business leaders will tell you that they don't do much at all. What they mean is that they have got their team and organisation to the point where it runs very efficiently on a day-to-day basis with the minimum of intervention from them. Everyone knows where the organisation is heading and what they have to do in order to get it there. Getting the organisation to that point is the tricky bit, and one that requires the leader to select the right people, set the right direction and agenda, persuade everyone of its worth, ensure everyone involved understands their role, and encourage them to give their very best in its pursuit. Over the next few chapters we will look more closely at these key aspects of leaderships, and the techniques that leaders use in practice.

Some leaders liken their role to that of a conductor of an orchestra. The musicians are excellent individually at what they do, and the conductor's job is to make sure that they are all playing the same piece, on time and in tune. Perhaps a better analogy is that of the captain of a rugby team. Martin Johnson, who captained England to World Cup victory in 2003, says that when he is on the pitch, if everything is going to plan his only job is to play the game to the best of his ability and to lead by example, offering constant encouragement along the way. The players know the game plan, have rehearsed key moves and work well together as a team. But if conditions change and players are facing the unexpected, the captain steps in to find a new way forward.

Being placed into a position of power does not make you a leader, and that is especially true of the modern business world. It is sometimes said that the essence of leadership is that a boss will say 'Go' while a leader will say 'Let's go'. And hopefully, people will follow, because they want to.

WHAT YOU NEED TO READ

▶ The average bookshop will not be short of books on leadership, which generally fall into three broad categories: relatively dry academic publications on leadership theory; more mainstream analyses of leadership styles; and books written about or by well-known business leaders. In the first category, Warren Bennis' *On Becoming A Leader* (Basic Books, 2009, other editions available) is mercifully readable and should be required reading for anyone hope to reach a leadership position. *The Leadership Challenge* by James Kouzes and Barry Posner (Jossey-Bass, 2008, 4th edn) is another important introduction to the subject and more information is available on the authors' website (www.leadershipchallenge.com)

▶ The view of which of the experienced-based memoirs are most helpful to aspiring leaders depends on your view of each individual leader, but *Winning* by Jack Welch (Harper Collins, 2005) is a great start.

▶ *History Lessons* by Jonathan Gifford (Marshall Cavendish, 2010) is an entertaining appraisal of leaders throughout history, from Gengis Khan to Winston Churchill, and contains some interesting views on the leadership qualities and abilities that are most successful.

▶ Abraham Zaleznik's article 'Managers and Leaders: Are They Different?' (1977) in the *Harvard Business Review* is considered a leadership classic and is essential reading if you want to seem well-informed on the subject. It is widely acclaimed as the seminal explanation of the distinction between a manager and a leader.

▶ More tips and views of what makes a successful leader can be found on the websites of well-known leadership writers, such as Tom Peters (www.tompeters.com) and John Adair (www .johnadair.co.uk).

IF YOU ONLY REMEMBER ONE THING

Leadership used to be about control but today it is about people – finding the best, giving them the resources and direction they need, and encouraging them to do their best.

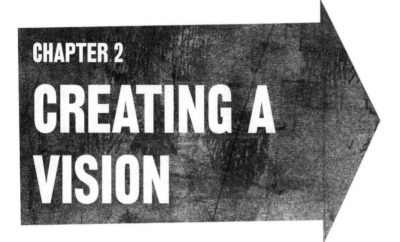

CHAPTER 2
CREATING A VISION

WHAT IT'S ALL ABOUT ➡

- ▶ The importance of a vision
- ▶ The power of a common enemy
- ▶ How to communicate the vision
- ▶ How to translate vision into performance

Setting a vision is the most fundamental thing a leader will do. Some would argue that it's the *only* important thing a leader will ever do, because it's up to the leader to decide where the organisation or group should be going, and up to everyone else to get them there. A destination or an outcome is vital to any group, whether it is a short-term or a long-term plan. Without a vision, there is simply no leadership, because if you don't know where you want to go, how can you expect anyone to follow?

IDENTIFYING A HIGHER PURPOSE

It is the responsibility of the leader to dictate the direction of the organisation or team they lead but, incredibly, this is something that many people in leadership positions in business fail to do – or if they do it, they fail to communicate their decision adequately to everyone else. According to research carried out by the Chartered Institute of Personnel and Development, only half of workers believe that their leader has a strategy. In other words, they have no idea what they are working towards – they have no understanding of a common goal. That is a risky state for a group of people to be in because it is part of the basic psychology of human beings to work together, but the best outcomes are achieved if they are working together in the belief that they are achieving something worthwhile. A shared purpose helps to create a strong team and fuels the motivation of everyone involved. If people are coming to work solely for the sake of eraning a wage, all they will give is the minimum possible effort.

The well-known management writer Warren Bennis argues in *The Secrets of Great Groups* that all organisations are built around a shared dream or motivating purpose. Bennis argues that the best visions are inspiring but realistic: 'Your team need not believe that it is literally saving the world. It is enough to feel it is helping people in need or battling a tough competitor. But simply punching a time clock doesn't do it.'

A vision does not have to be ground-breaking, original or innovative – indeed, the best visions are short, simple and straightforward. What is important is that the vision means something to everyone involved, that it describes an inspirational aim and that it translates easily into a realistic strategy that can be communicated simply to everyone. Sometimes, the art of a vision is that it articulates what has previously been understood, but left unsaid.

A good vision statement, well communicated, can work wonders. It can establish a common identity for a group of people that might do many different things. It underlines the worth of employees, enhances their self-respect and the value of what they are doing. It motivates people towards a common purpose and encourages them to take action in the right direction. A clear vision will also help to co-ordinate the actions and behaviour of a large group of people – in other words, it sets the direction.

THE DISTINCTION BETWEEN A VISION AND A MISSION STATEMENT

A vision is not the same as a mission statement (although in business you will sometimes hear the two used interchangeably). The point of a vision is that it is a distant and inspiring but ultimately achievable aim. The mission statement is set more in the present: A mission statement describes what a company does, but a vision describes where it is going.

Jack Welch argues that a mission statement should answer just one question: How do we intend to win in this business? While Welch was CEO at GE, the vision of the company was 'to be the most competitive enterprise in the world'. The company's mission statement, by contrast, was: 'To be number one or number two in every market.' In other words, the mission statement made the vision more specific.

Welch believes strongly that a mission statement can be as inspiring as a vision, but that is not always the case in practice. Apple's mission statement, for example is this: 'Apple designs Macs, the best personal computers in the world, along with OS X, iLife, iWork, and professional software. Apple leads the digital music revolution with its iPods and iTunes online store. Apple reinvented the mobile phone with its revolutionary iPhone and App Store, and has recently introduced its magical iPad which is defining the future of mobile media and computing devices.'

It's a very informative statement, but not one that is likely to get thousands of employees fired up with enthusiasm. But, of course, Apple's CEO Steve Jobs, is something of a genius at creating an atmosphere of excitement and anticipation around the company and as you would expect, his vision statements (which have changed and developed over the years) are spot on in the way they sum up the excitement of infinite possibility. There have been few better than this: 'Our vision is that we have just begun.'

It may sound simple in theory but coming up with a single shared vision that covers everything a team or group or company does can be very tricky indeed. It's relatively rare that a leader will devote enough time to thinking carefully about what the organisation is really trying to do and what that may mean to everyone involved, which is why many business 'mission statements' are little more than meaningless management-speak. But a thoughtful and meaningful vision that neatly explains what a company is all about is invaluable in focusing the minds of everyone who works there.

FAMOUS VISIONS

Some visions from businesses over the years have become part of modern history. The vision of Henry Ford, for example, was 'to democratise the automobile' – and that is something that he certainly achieved. Similarly, the vision of Boeing was to 'bring the world into the jet age', and again the company was extraordinarily successful in achieving that aim. NASA's vision in the 1960s was simple, but could hardly have been more inspiring: 'To put a man on the moon by the end of the decade.' The vision of Walt Disney was even simpler: 'To make people happy.'

An excellent recent example of a leader setting a mean-ingful vision for an organisation, which served its purpose in creating a common motivating goal for everyone, lies in London's bid to win the 2012 Olympic and Paralympic Games. The Bid team was a complex organisation, employing people with enormously diverse skills, from architects to transport consultants and security experts. Its aim was not in doubt – it was to win the Olympic Games for London in 2012. What the team lacked, though, was a single, coherent vision that could bring everyone in the organisation together – was its vision to build the best Olympic stadia, or the most efficient transport system, or to hold the most secure Games ever? The vision that the Committee eventually developed was to become the basis of its successful bid to win the Olympics for London: 'To stage inspirational games that capture the imagination of young people around the world and leave a lasting legacy.'

VISIONS THAT ADAPT TO CHANGE

Ideally, the leaders' vision should be aspirational, and remain reasonably relevant to the organisation even as it grows. But that is not to say that the vision will never change. One of the characteristics that set leaders apart from managers is that leaders are – and in fact, they must be – forward-looking. They seek out new opportunities, try to anticipate change and look ahead for potential risks. The nature of business means that the vision for a company may well change over time, but it still serves the same purpose – to bring everyone in the organisation together. In fact, a vision is even more vital in times of crisis and uncertainty, because it gives people a clear direction and target at a time when they most need it.

A good leader will constantly reassess the vision and make sure that it remains an inspiring target. In the very early days of Microsoft, the young Bill Gates said that his aim, and the vision of the company, was 'to put a computer on every desk, in every home'. What he meant was that he wanted to make the emerging technology as widely available as possible and affordable for everyone. Microsoft was a new company at the time, in a market that was only beginning to develop and which was not well understood by many. Gates' statement worked because it was an inspiring vision that gave everyone in the company, whatever their role, a clear and admirable target to aim for. They were doing something worthwhile.

WHO YOU NEED TO KNOW
Bill Gates

Bill Gates was born in 1955 in Seattle, Washington. He went to Harvard in 1973 and set up a software company the following year with Paul Allen, a friend from Prep School. By 1976 the company had developed the BASIC interpreter for one of the first microcomputers to be developed, and Gates dropped out of Harvard. For the next 20 years he was primarily responsible for product development at Microsoft. His personal wealth was rumoured to have exceeded $100 billion at the height of the dotcom boom during the late 1990s.

Opinions differ about Gates' leadership style, with some describing him as abrasive during his early years at Microsoft. His skill, though, undoubtedly lies in his ability to spot the potential of the swift advances in computer technology, and to make sure that Microsoft maintained its position at the front of the pack while the market expanded at breakneck speed.

Gates stepped down as Microsoft's CEO in 2000 and stopped working for the company full-time in 2008. He remains non-executive chairman of the company but dedicates his working life to the Bill and Melinda Gates Foundation, which distributes much of the fortune he made from Microsoft to charitable causes around the world.

Obviously Microsoft's vision statement has had to change over the years as personal computers became part of our everyday use at home and at work. The vision statement of the company today says it is to 'help people and businesses throughout the world to realise their full potential'. It's not as precise as Microsoft's early vision, but is more suited to the fast-changing world of information technology because it is non-specific. It allows for changing technology, but also allows the management of the company to decide exactly *how* they will help people and businesses throughout the world to realise their full potential.

WHO SAID IT

"Typically, a vision is specific enough to provide real guidance to people, yet vague enough to encourage initiative and to remain relevant under a variety of conditions."
– John Kotter (Harvard Professor)

THE POWER OF A COMMON ENEMY

Good leaders are arch manipulators of human emotions – and that is not necessarily a bad thing. Human emotions are a powerful force and if you can harness a little of their energy you have a much better chance of getting your message as a leader across. A vision for the organisation that appeals to basic human desires – the need for inclusion, for striving together towards a common goal (preferably one that is seen as noble and good) – has a good head start.

One of the most powerful motivating emotions, and one that is frequently harnessed by canny leaders (as well as by the occasional psychopathic dictator), is the power of a common enemy. Identifying a rival or 'enemy', or if you can't find an obvious one, inventing one, gives people a clear target to aim for, and if it is possible to articulate why your vision is better and more worthy than the enemy's, so much the better. It's by no means unusual for a company to have a vision of overtaking, or obliterating completely, a major rival. The vision statement of Honda during the 1970s, for instance, was to 'destroy Yamaha'; Nike's a few years later was 'to crush Adidas'. Other leaders have set an aspirational vision that was less combative, but still contained the unspoken promise that their aim was to overtake or better a rival. The vision of Stanford University in the US, for instance, was 'to be the Harvard of the West'.

Sometimes these feuds can seem to get out of hand – particularly when a leader begins to believe the vision to the extent that they lose sight of their real strategy. Nevertheless, some healthy rivalry can work wonders in motivating people to perform at their best. Steve Jobs, for instance, and Michael Dell, the CEO of Dell Computers, had a long-running public feud during the 1990s. Jobs accused Dell of making 'unimaginative beige boxes', while Dell said he would shut down Apple if he was its CEO, at a time when the company was struggling. When Apple's market capitalisation overtook Dell, Jobs wrote to all of his employees pointing out the fact.

But if the most vital task a leader will perform is in setting the direction of the organisation, their job does not end there. Leaders do not just set a vision, they bear responsibility for seeing it through.

COMMUNICATING THE VISION

The first step in achieving an outcome is making sure that everyone involved knows where they are going. Even the most inspirational vision ever formed will count for nothing unless it is properly communicated to everyone involved. Communicating the vision does not simply mean slapping a slogan on every memo or email, it means making sure that people understand where they are heading, why it's important and, crucially, they believe in its worth.

Communicating a vision takes time, patience and persistence. Even the most striking and memorable of visions will have to be repeated over and over before it begins to sink in and become part of the everyday furniture of the organisation – which should be the ultimate aim.

WHO SAID IT

"Good business leaders create a vision, articulate the vision, passionately own the vision, and relentlessly drive it to completion."
– Jack Welch

An excellent example of a company that has been built around its vision is the American low-cost airline Southwest. Set up in Texas in 1971 with the original aim of providing low-cost flights at a time when it was becoming more expensive to drive between cities in south west of the US because of rising petrol prices, Southwest is now one of the most profitable airlines in the world. The intention of its founders was to 'free the skies' – to provide low-cost travel, but while maintaining excellent customer service. Its vision and culture is particularly admirable because Southwest does not have what could be described as a formal vision statement, and yet the values of the business are ingrained in everything it does and widely accepted and followed by its employees.

Southwest's website says that its 'mission' is 'dedication to the highest quality of customer service delivered with a sense of warmth, friendliness, individual pride and company spirit'. The company has what it calls a 'golden rule' – that if you treat people in the way you would want to be treated yourself, everything else will fall into place. But not only is this idea repeated often on billboards and company literature, Southwest goes one step further and takes great pains to recruit people who fit into the corporate culture, irrespective of whether they have the right qualifications for the job (with the exception of technical posts and pilots, obviously). The company takes the view that they can teach the necessary skills but that the right attitude can't be learned. The vision is so much part of the company and the way it operates, and so much a part of the people who work there, that it is impossible to separate one from the other.

WHO YOU NEED TO KNOW
Herb Kelleher

Born in New Jersey in 1931, Herb Kelleher is the founder and chief executive of Southwest Airlines, the best-known budget airline in the US. Kelleher set up the airline in 1971 in the face of strong opposition and competition from existing airlines and over the space of the next 20 years established it as one of the most popular domestic airlines in the country. At the time it was set up, Southwest's business model was revolutionary – offering lower fares by cutting out the 'frill' services, and operating a point-to-point scheduling system rather than the 'hub' system used by most other airlines. Kelleher effectively revolutionised the way many airlines are run today.

The company, though, as become as well known for the way it treats its employees as for its business model. Southwest regularly wins awards as one of the most admired companies in America and Kelleher has been voted one of the top five business leaders in the US by *USA Today* and the best CEO in the US by *Fortune* magazine. Kelleher is best known for the corporate culture he created and championed at Southwest, which has

become legendary
in its insistence that no-one takes
themselves seriously, and for the view that
work should be fun. Kelleher has said
that Southwest hires people for their attitude
and not for their skills, as essential skills
can be taught but attitude cannot. He
has also said that his lesson for leadership
is to 'be humble, work harder than
anyone else, and serve your people'.
Kelleher retired as chairman of Southwest
in 2008, but still works with
the company.

Communicating the vision of a group or organisation is a job that will never really end. It takes persistence, constant repetition and requires the leader to muster up constant enthusiasm for something that they will have to repeat over and over again. It might become boring from time to time, but it is the leader's responsibility to keep the vision in the minds of everyone following, to shore up enthusiasm levels around the vision, and to encourage the formation of an organisational culture that is built around the vision.

Communicating the vision is not particularly difficult but it does require energy, commitment and persistence. It means repeating the vision as often as possible and in many formats, while always making it meaningful and interesting. Good leaders use a series of tactics in making sure that their vision is meaningful to everyone, and achieves the intention of motivating everyone.

MAKING IT MEANINGFUL

The first, and probably the most important lesson in communication, is to tell a story around the vision. We will come back again and again during this book to the importance of stories. People respond to the emotions of stories, and are more likely to understand and remember the message. Bill Gates' vision for Microsoft of 'a computer on every desk in every home' is, essentially, a story. When people hear it, they visualise their own home, or the home of someone they know or someone in need. They attach emotions to the message and as a result, will be more motivated to achieve the ultimate goal.

WHO SAID IT

"There's nothing more demoralizing than a leader who can't clearly articulate why we're doing what we're doing."
– **James Kouzes and Barry Posner (leadership academics)**

One of the dangers of setting a vision for an organisation or team in business is that it can become mired in business language or in figures that, in reality, mean little to the people involved. Too many visions in business are merely numbers, and this is because they are set by the senior team. Figures motivate the senior team because that is how they think of the business, but numbers mean little further down the organisation. There is nothing about a number that is inspirational. No-one gets out of bed every morning for the sake of a number. The trick is to turn a number into a story, and to create a goal that means something to everyone.

A good example of the challenges of communicating a vision in a way that makes it meaningful to everyone was seen in a small but ambitious recruitment consultancy in the UK. In 2002, the board of the company set a vision for its future, which was that within three years, the group should have achieved turnover of £50 million a year. This was an ambitious goal that would require double-digit organic growth each year for five years. But it was a clear goal. The board set about a comprehensive and thorough campaign of communication. Every internal memo and email to staff was stamped with the clear footnote: *50 million, 2005*. Banners went up in the office: *50 million, 2005*. At the regular team and company briefings the same mantra was repeated: *50 million, 2005*.

The company, as it turned out, was phenomenally successful in getting its message across. Ask anyone in the organisation – at any level – what the business' long-term aim was and you would get the same answer: '50 million, 2005'. But while it was clear that everyone understood the aim, the board noticed after six months or so that its results were not as good as they had hoped. Their people knew where they were heading, but were not getting themselves there anything like fast enough. So after some reflection, rather than asking their people what the aim was, they asked them a more basic question: '50 million what?' In return they inevitably got a blank stare. £50 million profit? £50 million turnover? No-one was sure. And how could anyone they get enthusiastic about something they didn't understand?

The problem was that the vision was meaningless to the people in the business. It was just a number and a date. And your life does not change because of a number. The answer was to translate '50 million, 2005' into something that meant something real and concrete for everyone in the company, and gave them something tangible to aim for. It might mean, for instance, that the business would move into a new office, in a better part of town. Or that level of growth would mean that many more managers would be needed, which meant a number of promotion opportunities. Or it might mean the potential for share options if the company went public in the future. Good visions are powerful things because they give a purpose to everyday life.

The second important lesson is to keep the message short, and repeat it over and over again. Leaders will spend a lot of time talking about the vision for their organisation and there will be different versions for different occasions. But the most effective version will be a short, concise and compelling one, which takes maybe no more than 30 seconds to repeat. As we've seen, some of the best-known, and therefore most effective, visions in business history have been short and to the point.

There is another advantage in taking the time to distil a vision down to its basics, because a leader will have to repeat it over and over again, in a variety of ways. There is no substitute for repetition when it comes to communicating the vision through all levels. Some visions fail simply because the people at the top get bored of repeating themselves. They have formed the vision, refined it and spent all of their days thinking about it – it's hardly surprising that some lose interest in repeating it to others, day in and day out. But constant repetition and rein-forcement is the only way that a vision will become understood, and that has to come from the top. This means, incidentally, behaving in a way that reinforces the vision as well as repeating it. The fastest way to lose cred-ibility, and therefore followers, is to say one thing and do another. A leader should epitomise the vision in every way – everything they do and say should back it up.

Modern forms of communication may have their difficul-ties, but one clear advantage is that it is possible to reach many people at once, relatively simply. A vision can be repeated often and reinforced constantly by taking advantage of electronic channels such as email, webcasts and intranets. But that should not be at the expense of frequent face-to-face reinforcement. Whenever people see the leader, they should know what he or she stands for and where they want to take the group. And while the vision message has to come from the leader, a lot of the communication legwork can and should be done by key people within the group. If leaders lower down an organisation enthusiastically buy into the vision, they will also spread the word.

MEASURING UNDERSTANDING

It's always a good idea to test whether your efforts are reaping rewards and in this case, whether the vision is properly established in the organisation and understood by everyone. Again, testing understanding among followers is something that is frequently neglected in business, the rationale usually being that either it is too time-consuming or that it is too difficult.

Particularly effective leaders tend to go out of their way to find out what their followers think of their leadership and of what the organisation as a whole is doing. We will discuss some of the common techniques used to encourage a two-way conversation in Chapter 3, but a useful way of measuring the level of understanding of something – such as the vision – throughout an organisation is to use the T test.

The T test asks a series of questions of the management at the top of the organisation (on the basis that the important messages originate from them, so it is important that they have a full understanding of the issues), and then asks the same questions of someone from each level down the centre of the organisation. In a medium-sized sales company, for example, this might mean the company board (the T's horizontal), and then an executive that does not sit on the board, a regional manager, team leader, a member of the sales team and a secretary or receptionist (the T's vertical). The answers from each of these people will give the leader a thorough picture of how well the vision is known and understood (and accepted) throughout the organisation. An inconsistent response should tell the leader that not everyone is pulling in the same direction.

The T-test is useful because it helps a leader measure the 'softer' side of business performance, such as employee engagement or the understanding within a team of a concept (or, in this case, a vision). We will talk more of managing performance in later chapters, but a series of 12 questions, asked of people along the horizontal and vertical T lines, can help a leader assess understanding of the vision, and whether everyone has a common aim, and everything they need to achieve it:

- ► What is the overall company objective?
- ► What are the immediate business priorities?
- ► What are you doing to contribute towards these?
- ► How could you contribute more?
- ► How could your colleagues contribute more?
- ► How is the company doing overall?
- ► How could the company do better?
- ► What is good about the company?
- ► What gets in the way of progress?
- ► How good is communication within the company?
- ► What's morale like?
- ► What can be done to create a motivating environment?

Once the leader is sure that everyone has a common understanding of the vision, the next step is to translate the vision into performance.

BREAKING DOWN THE VISION INTO GOALS

So you have a vision, and a vision that people are willing to buy into and, with luck, that they are well aware of and understand. But how are you going to get there? A vision is nothing if it is not executed, and executed successfully. And this is the great test of a leader.

Once they have set the vision, everything a leader does is essentially focused on persuading people to follow that vision – we will discuss many of these activities, from building a team to managing performance and motivating people, in the coming chapters. It is essential that a leader is able to persuade people to buy into the vision because without that commitment, there is little chance of long term success. People can be forced or encouraged to perform in the short term, but long-term commitment and performance requires much more – it requires people to be motivated by their need for achievement, belonging, recognition and a sense of being part of something bigger than themselves. When a leader asks people to follow, what they are essentially asking is whether the leader's vision is worthy of their commitment. The vision lies at the centre of everything.

The first step for a leader is to persuade people that the vision is achievable. This is where much can be learned from the approach of world-class athletes and elite sportsmen and women. Champions have big dreams but they also have very detailed plans. The best know how to break down their ambitions into a series of achievable and understandable stages, which bring the vision, step by step, within reach.

For example, imagine that a young athlete has a dream of winning an Olympic Gold medal in, say, the men's 400 metres at the 2016 Games. This is the ultimate goal – the 'outcome goal'. But what will it take to win that gold medal? In order to win, the runner needs to complete the 400 metres in the fastest time. That means beating the best 400 metres athletes in the world. In 2010, the world record for the men's 400 metres was held by Michael Johnson, at 43.18 seconds (which was set in 1999). That means that the 'performance goal' – the time or score that will be necessary to achieve the outcome – will be, to be on the safe side, 43 seconds. The perform- ance goal is set because it maximises your chances of achieving the outcome goal, and converts the vision into a numerical target, which in the world of business may be money, or units of sales, or years. The performance goal is an accurate measure of what needs to be done in order to achieve the outcome goal.

Finally come the 'process goals', which are the tasks and skills that the athlete will need to work on in order to achieve the performance goal. Process goals cover the actions that the athlete needs to perfect in order to reach the performance goal. In the case of a 400 metres runner, this will include the start, the bend running technique, stamina, race tactics, diet and nutrition and mental performance. The process goals might also be marked by a series of success points along the way, which show that the athletes is improving and heading towards the performance goal and outcome goal. This might mean, for instance, running a personal best of 44 seconds, or winning a regional or national championship. Athletes tend to spend most of their time concentrating on the process goals, with their eye always on the outcome goal as motivation. The process goals are by no means set in stone and should be under constant reassessment to make sure that they will lead the athlete to the outcome goal.

WHO SAID IT

"A successful individual typically sets his next goal somewhat but not too much above his last achievement. In this way, he steadily raises his level of aspiration."

– Kurt Lewin (US psychologist)

APPLYING PROCESS GOALS TO BUSINESS

In business terms, the outcome goal – which is essentially the vision set by the leader – provides the passion and desire necessary to persuade people to push themselves through the process goals. It is relatively simple for athletes and other sportsmen to break down their outcome goal into the clear stages that become the process goals. For leaders in business, breaking down the outcome goal into the detailed, day-to-day work that will get the organisation to the goal takes some careful thought and planning and as a result, is one that business leaders can tend to neglect. Many businesses spend too long thinking about the outcome goal and performance goal, but too little time on the process goals.

Often the problem is an over-complication of the messages around the process goals. A study by Cranford Business School found that 90% of business leaders knew exactly what they needed to do (i.e. they had clear outcome goals and performance goals), but only 20% had executed their plan effectively (in other words, the process goals were not working).

A common problem is that business leaders tend to overload their team with priorities. The more priorities people are asked to concentrate on, the less likely it is that any will be achieved. For that reason, leaders who want to get a message across clearly and make sure that everyone is working efficiently in the same direction, tend to focus on only three process goals. They identify three priorities for everyone to concentrate on – that might include, for instance, making sure that customer calls are answered within xx seconds, or improving staff retention rates by x%. The underlying psychological rationale is that two priorities are probably not enough to make a real difference to the outcome, whereas if there are four or more priorities not everyone will concentrate equally on all of them and the overall impact will be lessened. Three is a powerful number – enough to make a difference, and easy to remember.

Armed with a simple but inspiring vision, which they are careful to keep under constant reassessment to be sure that it remains relevant, the role of the leader has begun. The function of a leader from here on in – in encouraging high performance, building a strong team, motivating and inspiring their people – will all be built on the foundations of their vision.

WHAT YOU NEED TO READ

▶ The business writer Jim Collins is particularly interesting on the subject of vision in leadership. His books include *Built to Last: Successful Habits of Visionary Companies* (Harper Collins, 2005) and *How the Mighty Fall: And Why Some Companies Never Give In* (Random House Business, 2009).

▶ Bill Gates' two books, *The Road Ahead* (Viking, 1995) and *Business at the Speed of Thought* (Penguin, 1999) show how he applied and adapted his vision for Microsoft in practice. The *Autobiography* of Lee Iocacca (Bantam, 1986), the former chief executive of Chrysler, is another detailed and readable account of an excellent business leader in action during a time when his business was undergoing a major transformation.

▶ An interesting profile of and interview with Herb Kelleher of Southwest Airlines can be seen on *The Leader Network* (www.leadernetwork.org)

IF YOU ONLY REMEMBER ONE THING

A leader cannot be a leader without a clear and inspiring vision. The vision is the 'glue' that transforms a collection of individuals into a group who are intent on collective effort in order to achieve a common aim.

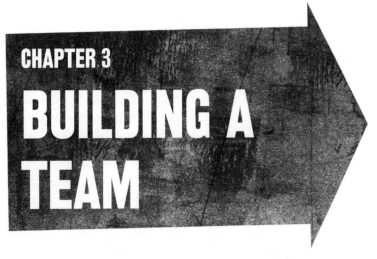

CHAPTER 3
BUILDING A TEAM

WHAT'S IT ALL ABOUT ▶

► Why teams matter
► The power of collective effort
► How to recruit the right people
► Ways of transforming people into teams

It is often assumed that a team is only as good as its leader. That is not strictly true. A bad leader can certainly impose untold harm on a team of people, but a successful team or business is not successful purely because of its leader. Success requires a team effort, and the responsibility for creating, building and maintaining the team lies firmly with the leader.

The management writer Jim Collins talks about performance in business in terms of 'getting the right people on the bus'. This is an analogy that frequently crops up in the discussion about leadership. The bus is the company, obviously, and it is the job of the leader to get it moving. The leader decides where the bus is going and how it's going to get there. But Collins argues that the thing that sets great companies apart from the rest is that they start not with the 'where' but with the 'who'. They start by getting the right people on the bus, in the right seats. In other words, first they deal with the people, and then they start on the direction.

Collin's argument is that if a leader has the right people on board, the business is better able to adapt to change, to take advantage of opportunities and to ride out any difficulties. If the leader has the best people on board they are more likely to be self-motivated because they are working with other great people. However good the vision of the leader, he adds, if there are mediocre people on board the best that can be produced is a mediocre result.

WHO SAID IT

"We cling to the myth of the Lone Ranger, the romantic idea that great things are usually accomplished by a larger-than-life individual working alone, despite evidence to the contrary. Michelangelo worked with a group of 16 to paint the ceiling of the Sistine Chapel."
– **Warren Bennis**

Creating a team that performs well is one of the most important things a leader will do. But this in itself requires a wide range of skills. It means that the leader must have the emotional intelligence to understand their own strengths and weaknesses as well as the strengths and weaknesses of them around them, so they can look for people who will fill in the skills gaps in the team, while complementing its strengths. Then they must make sure that the processes to find these elusive people are up to scratch. But that's not all. The leader must also create an environment that the people they want to attract will want to join – and not want to leave. All in all, team building is a tall order.

The problem for aspiring leaders is that western cultures, as a whole, are not particularly well trained in the art of team building. With the exception of team sports, throughout most of our lives we are encouraged to compete individually and not to collaborate. As students were are trained from our teenage years to be independent and work problems out for ourselves. Building and maintaining a strong team spirit, in other words, is not something that is going to come naturally to many western business leaders. It is something that most have to work very hard at.

THE POWER OF COLLECTIVE EFFORT

There is a popular US saying that 'none of us is as smart as all of us' which, in a nutshell, sums up the modern approach to leadership. As opposed to the historical command-and-control approach to leadership, modern leadership is a much more collaborative effort, where the leader brings together a group of people with the right skills and attitude, sets them a stretching target, and continues to motivate them in towards the achievement of it. This is particularly true of business leaders, who inevitably operate in a complex environment that demands an enormous range of skills and diverse experience. No leader can do everything, but their power lies in recruiting, retaining and motivating the right people who, collectively, achieve the best possible performance.

Some of the most well-known and influential work on the power of collective effort has been carried out by the leadership writer and academic Warren Bennis. He argued that most problems are far too complex to be solved by just one person, and that the best chance of success in business comes when you gather together a wide variety of people from various backgrounds and with contrasting and complementary skills, who work together to solve a problem or achieve a common purpose. He called this collection of talent 'Great Groups'.

WHO YOU NEED TO KNOW

Warren Bennis

Born in the US in 1925, Warren Bennis is one of the most widely-respected leadership writers in the world. Bennis studied at Antioch College in the 1940s following his military service, later working as a professor at the MIT Sloan School of Management. In the 1960s he moved into a more practical leadership role as provost of the State

University of New York, and then president of the University of Cincinnati. He returned to teaching in 1979 at the University of Southern California, but has also worked as an advisor to four US Presidents and consultant to many large companies.

Bennis is often credited with introducing leadership studies into the mainstream with a paper published in the Harvard Business Review in 1961 on his 'revisionist theory of leadership'. He has written 27 books, including *Co-leaders: The Secrets of Great Partnerships*, *Leaders* and *On Becoming a Leader*, and is consistently ranked as one of the most significant figures in leadership studies in the world.

Bennis' work on teams, or 'great groups' as he called them, has been particularly influential. By studying an eclectic mix of teams that had achieved extraordinary results, Bennis was able to argue that one of the key functions of a successful leader was 'meticulous recruiting'. It was the leader's ability to collect together extraordinary talent and making sure that it achieved what it was meant to achieve, that made the difference between success and failure, he reasoned. 'These groups made the leaders great,' said Bennis. 'The leaders I studied were seldom the brightest or best in the group, but neither were they passive players. They were connoisseurs of talent, more like curators than creators.'

As part of his work, Bennis studied some of the most successful companies and organisations of the late twentieth century – collections of people who collectively produced ideas or products that changed the face of their industry, or even of the world, and which included the Manhattan Project that produced the first atomic bomb, and the early innovations of Apple in the days when it was developing its Mac computers. He then attempted to identify the characteristics that had underpinned their achievements.

This research led Bennis to set out ten principles that he believed were common to all 'great groups'. The first of these was that they shared a dream, to the extent that they were willing to abandon their individual egos in pursuit of it. This is the vision, set by the leader, which we discussed in Chapter 2. A vision that is stretching and challenging and yet attainable is highly motivational to team members. Bennis also recognised that creating an environment where the team is striving against a common enemy (even if the enemy is invented) or for an admirable purpose, is a strong added incentive. This is why setting a vision is so fundamental to leadership – it is the fuel on which the team will run.

RECRUITING EXCELLENCE

A leader needs great people, and that means seeking out and attracting the best talent they can find for the business, as well as encouraging the best performance possible from the existing workforce. Experienced leaders maintain that finding and recruiting the best possible people for the business is one of the most important things they will ever do. Jack Welch, the former CEO of General Electric, argues that selecting the right people is one of only three jobs that he had to do at the multinational (the other two being allocating capital resources and spreading ideas quickly).

The quality and ability of its employees (its intellectual capital) forms a major part of the value of many modern businesses – the multi-billion dollar values placed on Google, Microsoft and Apple being a case in point. Successive studies have shown that 'recruiting excellence' – meaning well-planned recruitment that supports the business plan by placing the right people in the right roles – can have a positive impact on the market value of a business and on its profits. Finding and keeping the right people is critical to a company's success, and yet it is rather easier said than done.

There is a growing trend among some companies to recruit for attitude rather than for skill. Sir Richard Branson's Virgin Group and Southwest Airlines are two of the best-known proponents of this approach, both taking the view that while many skills can be learnt, attitude cannot. This is becoming an increasingly popular view and is an important point to bear in mind when recruiting, as it is remarkably easy to focus purely on skills, qualifications and experience when some of the most important competencies for success are attitude and behaviour.

There are two stages to recruitment: attraction and selection. Potential applicants have to be attracted to the company and want to work there, and then the company must chose the applicants who are best suited to the organisation's culture and values. The leader holds ultimate responsibility for both stages – they set the vision for the business, and the corporate culture that will (hopefully) make it the sort of organisation that people want to work for, and they will be responsible for (either directly or indirectly) the recruitment of new people to the team. As a business grows, leaders often find that much of the responsibility for recruitment is taken by someone else, whether that is an internal HR department or an outside recruitment agency. Even so, the leader still bears a great responsibility – for specifying what skills and candidates they are looking for, for making sure that any new people fit in well with the company's culture and values, and for identifying areas where the company's skills need strengthening. In other words, the recruitment strategy should closely align to the overall strategy of the business, which is set by the leader. That means that leaders step away from the recruitment process at their peril.

A basic requirement for building an effective team is the ability to assess candidates. Any leader, at some stage in their career, will be called on to interview potential recruits. Leaders must be good at many things and not all of them are instinctive or based on common sense. Interviewing skills is a classic example. It is an important skill and one that is almost always learned rather than innate. It's remarkably easy to be bad at interviewing – many people are. They talk too much, fail to prepare adequately, don't take notes or make premature decisions based on instinct, rather than a cool assessment of whether the candidate will be a valuable member of the team. An interview should achieve three aims: It should confirm the candidate's suitability for the job; it should imprint the candidate with a positive impression of the organisation because even if you don't want them to work for you, they shouldn't leave the room ready to run down the company to anyone who will listen; and it should make sure that the candidate is left with a realistic and honest view of the organisation and of the job in question.

CONDUCTING AN INTERVIEW

There are ten golden rules to conducting a good interview:

1. **Prepare.** Take at least ten minutes to review the candidate's CV before the interview, and note down any questions that occur to you, or areas that need to be looked at in more detail. A good candidate will come armed with a list of questions for you, so you need to be on your toes. What specific skills are you looking for? Are you looking for a particularly personality 'type' who will fit in well with the rest of the team? How are you going to tease out that information? Don't expect to wing it.

2. **Stick to your agenda.** A good interview will have a clear structure, which will probably run something like this:
   - ▶ *Greet the candidate*
   - ▶ *Explain the format of the interview and how long it is likely to take*
   - ▶ *Ask your questions*
   - ▶ *Describe the post and the organisation (doing this before asking your questions increases the risk that you will be told what the candidate thinks you want to hear)*
   - ▶ *Ask the candidate if they have any questions*
   - ▶ *Close*

   Sticking to a clear framework will ensure that you stay in control of the situation. It's usually dangerous to assume that you will automatically be in control, just because you are the interviewer. Most people expect an interview to last about an hour so it's generally best to say that it will last 45 minutes, giving you the option to end it a few minutes early without appearing unprofessional, or overrunning if you think you haven't heard enough.

3. **Choose the right location.** Gareth Jones, the former HR director at the BBC, recommends conducting the interview on reasonably neutral ground, on the basis that interviewing in your own office can be intimidating and the average meeting room can be depressing and characterless. He regularly interviews candidates in a café or pub, which has the dual

benefit of encouraging the candidate to relax a little, but also lowers their natural guard so you are more likely to get an honest approximation of their personality. Experienced interviewers also recommend that you and the interviewee sit on chairs that are set at right angles to each other, rather than face to face, and that you avoid sitting behind a desk, which can be interpreted as confrontational, if at all possible.

4. **Respect their nerves.** You should expect an interviewee to be nervous – it's only natural. However tempting it might be to ratchet up the stress levels to see how they cope (or for your own power-crazed gratification, in which case you're probably beyond any help this book can give), there is little to be gained from that approach. There are unlikely to be any situations as artificial and stress-inducing than a job interview during their working life with the organisation. It's a one-off. So be friendly and try to build some rapport.

5. **Ask the right questions.** Experienced interviewers generally take the view that a competency-based approach – whereby you look for specific evidence of the candidate's behaviour in certain situations – is the most productive line of questioning to adopt. Your interview planning should have highlighted what skills and abilities you are looking for, so questions about specific events in their professional life so far, and how they dealt with a merger, or cost-cutting

programme, for instance, should be framed in order to tease out a better idea of what they might have to offer. Ask open questions ('Tell me about..'.) rather than closed questions that only require a yes or no answer, and keep your questions short and simple – one point at a time. Hypothetical scenarios tend to illicit a textbook answer, so avoid them unless you are specifically looking for someone creative.

6. **Get them to talk.** It's an interview, not a conversation. As the interviewer, you should only be aiming to talk for about 30% of the session. Leave the rest to the candidate. But be prepared to politely cut off a determined talker, or someone who is straying too far from the point. Not everyone enjoys talking about themselves and interviewees will naturally be nervous, so the occasional 'mmm' and 'aha' will encourage them to offer more about themselves.

7. **Listen.** Various studies of interview situations have shown that around 40% of interviewers tend to make up their mind about a candidate within 20 minutes of meeting them. Half of those had reached a definitive conclusion within ten minutes. It's natural to make a snap decision about someone based on their clothes, or handshake or even a careless nervous slip in the first few minutes. The danger is that your initial impression will colour your judgment

and you will stop listening to what they have to say. Give everyone a fair hearing – you might find a hidden gem.

8. **Take notes.** Don't expect to miraculously remember everything about every candidate you meet – the chances are that if you are interviewing more than a handful, they will begin to blur into one. Jot down key things that strike you during the interview, and take 15 minutes or so at the end of the day to make sense of your notes.

9. **Play the attraction game.** An interview is as much about selling the company, and your skills as a leader, as it is about selecting the right people for your team. If a candidate has a bad experience at an interview, or comes away with the impression that the company is chaotic, or your leadership skills are less than impressive, they are not likely to keep their views to themselves. Even if you would not want them working for you, they might put off talented candidates from applying in the future.

10. **Close the meeting professionally.** Always take the time to explain the next step in the recruitment process and when the candidate can expect to hear from you again. Try not to be vague about dates. It's rarely a good idea to make a snap judgment and offer someone a job on the spot, but be encouraging and give positive feedback if you think it is warranted.

THE BEST FOR THE JOB

Some people are excellent at interviews; others are not. Selecting the best from a line-up of bright candidates can be a minefield, and it's usually a good idea to think carefully about your first instinct. Even if one person has outshone the rest that does not necessarily mean that they are the best person for you, or for the job. Good recruiters take time to review what they were looking for in the first place, and ask themselves some hard questions before they make a final decision: is the candidate over-qualified and likely to become bored? If I offer the job, how likely are they to accept?

The recruitment process is a difficult and challenging one but it is by no means over once you have a good candidate in place. Unless the candidate fits into the organisation, and feels involved with it, they are unlikely to offer their best. The development of the 'insider feeling' – the sense of involvement with the company that encourages people to give their best, as we will discuss in much more detail in later chapters – should begin early, and at least as soon as a job offer is made and preferably earlier than that, during the initial interview. People want to work for leaders they like, respect and admire.

With a little work, it is possible to begin evolving a sense of inclusiveness even before a new recruit has joined the business, by inviting them to meet colleagues socially and by including them in (non-confidential) communication. Once they have joined the company, the induction process should be well-planned (this is something that many companies overlook) and timely. How many people have turned up for work on their first day to find that their line manager is on holiday? Or are asked to take an induction session three months after their joining date? You can't expect anyone to become a valuable part of a team entirely on their own – it takes work to get the best out of people.

TRANSFORMING PEOPLE INTO TEAMS

With luck and more than a little judgment, a leader can gather talented people around them with the necessary skills to propel the company forward at a pace. But the simple fact of employing talented people does not make them a team who will work together effectively. A team is a team when every member trusts everyone else to do their job properly – and no member wants to let the others, or their leader, down.

If you distil down all of the research and studies into leadership and teams, it is possible to identify a few key drivers that lie behind any successful team. By concentrating on those key elements, a leader can gain a head start in encouraging team performance. Put simply, successful teams have a collective purpose or aim, all the resources they need, and the trust but relatively distant support of their leader.

The management writer James MacGregor Burns argued that the success of a leader depends on their ability to encourage performance from a team of people that is greater than they would produce individually. It's a collaborative and mutual approach to leadership where people encourage each other, understand what they are doing and why, and take ownership of their work. This style of leadership, which has become the norm in recent years, requires the leader to develop 'soft' skills such as an ability to read people and situations, excellent communication techniques, as well as a degree of emotional intelligence.

WHO YOU NEED TO KNOW
James MacGregor Burns

An American writer born in 1918, James MacGregor Burns was well known as a biographer of several US Presidents before he turned his attention to leadership studies. His biography of Roosevelt won a Pulitzer Prize and the National Book Award in 1971.

Burns is best known for separating the study of leadership into two contrasting ideas. He identified the more traditional study of leadership, which focused on the personality traits and behaviour of leaders and their ability to direct and persuade followers to do what they wanted them to do, as 'transactional leadership'. The other form of leadership identified by Burns, with which his name became synonymous, was 'transformational leadership', which concentrated on the interaction of leaders and their team. Transactional and transformational leadership, he argued, could not happen at the same time.

Burns argued that 'transformational leadership occurs when one or more persons engage with others in such a way that leaders and followers raise one another to higher levels of motivation and morality'. The leader encourages and motivates their followers (or team) to perform at their best through a series of actions, including tying the follower's identity to the vision and collective identity of the organisation, and encouraging followers to take greater responsibility for their work and their actions. Burns believed strongly that transformational leadership changed the lives of people, in terms of their aspirations and values, and the nature of organisations. Transformational leaders, he argued, tend to lead through example and by explaining their vision and goals for the group in an inspiring way.

TEAM THEORY

It's not necessarily the case that a team of highly skilled people will always work effectively together as a team. A team needs people who are good at getting on with others, as well as people who are good at what they do.

The UK academic Dr Meredith Belbin carried out some interesting research into teamwork in the 1980s, in which he identified a phenomenon that he labelled 'The Apollo Syndrome', where a team made up of highly capable individuals manages to perform poorly collectively. His research showed that a team that was selected on the basis of high analytical skills which, purely from the ability of individual members, should have outperformed others, consistently finished behind teams made up of less technically capable individuals. Belbin found that the team with the best analytical skills tended to argue between themselves about the best course of action, had trouble making decisions and failed to co-ordinate their actions effectively. Belbin's study is taken as a warning that it is rarely a good idea to form a team from the most intelligent candidates available – some thought is needed into the way the team dynamic will operate.

This and other studies of teams over the years have concluded that members of high-performing teams tend to follow two distinct sets of behaviour. These are usually described as task-related roles and relationship-related roles. Task-related roles are those that help to get a particular job done, such as delegating or setting targets or monitoring progress. When a team is placed under pressure, the task-related roles will generally emerge first and will dominate in order to tackle the immediate job in hand. But it is the relationship-related roles that actually keep the team together. These roles look for common ground between team members and sorting out any disagreements between them. If either the task-related roles or the relationship-related roles dominate too strongly for too long, the usual outcome is that the team falls apart – in the first case because the team relationships break down, and in the second because the team concentrates on getting on with each other, at the expense of effective action.

Creating a successful team is often a case of trial and error, and any group of people need time to gel. Teams tend to pass through several stages of development, when they first form or when new members join. These are sometimes called:

> ▶ The *forming* stage, when the team is put together.
> ▶ The *storming* stage, when they discuss or argue about what they need to do and how they should do it.
> ▶ The *norming* stage, when they agree on how they will work together to achieve the aim.
> ▶ The *performing* stage, when the team exclusively focuses on the task.

Not all teams will progress steadily through each stage. For some, the team will fall apart at the storming stage simply because the team members cannot agree on the best way forward. Others may try to skip straight from forming to performing, because they are under pressure to produce results or perhaps too many team members can't cope with the inevitable conflict that comes with the storming stage. The point for leaders to remember, though, is that every new team – and every team that takes on a new member – needs time to go through the forming stage before it becomes effective. They need time to settle down and become a team.

WHO SAID IT

"Coming together is a beginning. Keeping together is progress. Working together is success."
– Henry Ford

KNOW YOUR PEOPLE

This all helps to illustrate why leaders need excellent people and situation-sensing skills, and why it is absolutely essential that a leader takes the time to know and understand their followers.

The importance of knowing your people will come up time and again in this book, simply because it is the essential foundation of modern leadership. It is impossible for a leader to coax the best performance out of their people unless they understand what makes them tick. As we will see in the following chapters, people are prepared to volunteer extra effort if they feel that the leader treats them as a 'human being', rather than as a 'human doing' a task. Knowing your people is essential to motivating them, to assessing and improving their performance, and in persuading them to follow where you lead.

Surprisingly, given the general perception that the military tends to favour command-and-control leadership, officer training lays great emphasis on the important of knowing your men and making an effort to mix with them regularly in order to assess the level of morale. Major General Patrick Cordingley, who led the Desert Rats during the first Gulf War, makes the point that you cannot be a successful military leader without knowing the strengths and weaknesses of your men, and playing to those abilities in order to get the best out of them. But placed in situations of stress – and nothing is as stressful as a battlefield – people will react differently and it is only by mixing with them regularly that a leader can see the stress points and work to reassure them before too much damage is done.

There is no short cut to reaching the point where you know your followers well – good leaders take the time to talk to their people informally, and are genuinely interested in them. They also offer information about themselves, albeit selectively, as this is the most efficient way of encouraging people to talk about themselves. Probably the best test of whether a leader knows a member of their team is whether they are able to buy them an inexpensive gift that touches them personally. It shows that the leader knows what music they like to listen to, or their favourite football team. It shows that the leader has taken time to understand where they have come from and what they are shaped by.

TEAMSHIP RULES

Ultimately, the leader must have the courage and confidence to step back and let the team get on with the job. This requires mutual trust between the leader and team, and between team members themselves. The reality in business is that most teams are over-managed and under-led. The best leaders leave space for initiative, and for people to take ownership of ideas.

A valuable tactic in encouraging this environment of trust and respect is for the leader to delegate the responsibility for setting the rules of behaviour to the team, rather than imposing their own rules from above.

Sir Clive Woodward successfully developed this idea while he was coach of the England rugby team in the run-up to their World Cup win in Australia in 2003. His argument was that if the rules were set and agreed on by the players themselves, they were more likely to be followed and seen as a level of professionalism that they naturally upheld, rather than rules that were only there to be followed.

Woodward called these the 'teamship rules'. The idea began during his first meeting with the team and coaches at their training camp. Every day began with a 10 am meeting in a conference room, before the team headed out on to the practice pitch. On that first morning, Woodward waited in the room as the players trickled in one after another, some of them on their mobile phones. By 10.15 am, everyone had arrived. Woodward was quietly irritated, but carried on to explain his vision for the team; it was to be the best rugby team in the world, and to prove it by winning the Rugby World Cup.

One he had set out his vision, he asked the players to create a set of standards around their behaviour that would be agreed and followed by all of them. He suggested that they should discuss between themselves what the rules should be on timekeeping, and on the use of mobile phones. If he agreed with the rules they came up with, he would sign them off and they would be set in stone. The next morning, the players came back with the suggestion that everyone should be 10 minutes early for every meeting, and that mobile phones should only be used in players' bedrooms while they were at the training camp, and in their cars.

These rules were, in fact, stricter than Woodward would have imposed himself and from that point onwards, they were strictly adhered to by the team – and self-monitored, as any player who broke a rule would receive endless teasing from the rest of the team. The players had soon developed a collection of behavioural rules, covering everything from their personal appearance off the pitch to what should and should not be said in press interviews, which became the players' manual and encouraged a level of professional behaviour that was a matter of pride for the entire team.

This concept has been successfully translated to the business environment, where employees are asked to suggest codes of behaviour around, for example, what they wear to work, the preferred telephone manner to clients and customers, how they behave at social events and how the holiday rotas should be organised. Teamship rules work because the team has ownership of them – it feels different doing something that you have all agreed among yourselves, than it does doing something because someone has told (or ordered) you to. The quality of the teamship rules that are suggested by followers will generally be connected to the vision that is set by the leader – if the vision is sufficiently inspiring and aspirational (to be the best), the behavioural code will be equally world-class. Asking the team to set its own code of conduct also has the added bonus of clearing one more task from the leader's desk.

ENGAGEMENT

Many leaders find delegation incredibly difficult and assume that they hold responsibility for solving every problem and coming up with every new idea. A leader who does not delegate can be dangerous for an organisation, and it inhibits innovation and the ability of its people to think for themselves. A great team, consisting of good people with complementary skills who know where they are going and why, should make delegation a natural process. Great leaders know how to build a good team, but also know that in order to work effectively, teams have to be trusted to get on with the job without constant interference.

The ultimate aim for a leader in building a successful team is to create a group of people who are so committed to what they are doing that they will contribute their full effort to getting it done. The leader plays a significant role in this process, not just in creating the team but in motivating it over time and inspiring people to do their best, as we will discuss in the following chapters. In business the phenomenon of fully committed people working together in a business is frequently referred to as 'employee engagement'.

Engaged employees are seen as vital to performance because they contribute all of their efforts to performance, and so have a positive impact on results. Their rate of production is higher so they are more profitable, they are more focused on customers and clients, and they are less likely to leave the company. Disengaged employees, however, are potential poison for a team performance because do not perform well themselves and they sap the motivation of others. The consultancy Gallup has done some important and very well-known work on employee engagement, and estimates that, on average there are two engaged employees to every disengaged employee in the working population. Good leaders are constantly working to improve this ratio – Gallup's work suggests that the most successful businesses in the world show a ratio of at least eight or nine engaged employees to each disengaged employee.

ASSESSING EMPLOYEE ENGAGEMENT

Gallup devised a series of questions which are designed to assess the level of engagement within business (which Gallup calls Q12 Meta Analysis). These questions are an excellent way of assessing whether a team is motivating and working well together – the aim should be for each team member to answer 'yes' to at least seven of the following questions:

- ▶ I know what is expected of me at work.
- ▶ I have the materials and equipment I need to do my work.
- ▶ I have the opportunity to do what I do best every day at work.
- ▶ In the past seven days, I have received recognition or praise for doing good work.
- ▶ My supervisor, or someone at work, seems to care about me as a person.

► There is someone at work who encourages my development.
► At work, my opinion seems to count.
► The mission or purpose of the organisation makes me feel that my job is important.
► My associates or fellow employees are committed to doing quality work.
► I have a best friend at work.
► In the past six months, someone at work has talked to me about my progress.
► In the past year, I have had opportunities at work to learn and grow.

As we will see in the following chapters, good leaders concentrate their efforts on making sure that as many of their people as possible can answer 'yes' to these questions. The success of every team, and every business, depends on the ability of the leader to encourage consistently high performance and maintain a constant level of motivation – a level of motivation that is maintained even when the leader is absent.

A leader cannot be everywhere. All he or she can do is make sure that they have the best people in the right role, that they know what to do and have the resources and training they need to do it. At some point, the leader must step back and let the team do their job – and crucially, trust the team to do their job.

WHAT YOU NEED TO READ

▶ Warren Bennis' research on 'great groups' is perhaps a little outdated but is nevertheless an important milestone in the study of teamwork. His research can be seen in an article in Leader to Leader (No 3, 1997), *The Secrets of Great Groups* (www.leadertoleader.org).

▶ Jim Collins discusses some of his views on 'getting the right people on the bus' in his book, *Good to Great: Why Some Companies Make the Leap ... and Others Don't* (Harper Collins, 2005). Collins also has a website that discusses many of his ideas: www.jimcollins.com.

▶ Dr Meredith Belbin's work on teams is a little on the academic side, but still fascinating. Particularly interesting is *Management Teams – Why They Succeed or Fail*, (Butterworth Heinemann, 2010, 3rd edn) and more information can be found at www.belbin.com

▶ For more on Gallup's Meta Analysis, go to the employee engagement article under the Management Consulting, Functional Practices section on the Gallup website (www.gallup.com). There is a more extensive discussion in two books published by the firm: *First, Break All The Rules* and *12: The Elements of Great Managing*.

▶ Successful recruitment is a subject in itself, and again there is certainly no shortage of reading material available. At the risk of blowing our own trumpet, *Recruiting Excellence* by Jeff Grout and Sarah Perrin (McGraw Hill Professional, 2005) is an excellent place to start. *Winning the Talent War* by Charles Woodruffe (John Wiley, 1999) and *Topgrading* by Bradford Smart (Portfolio, 1999) both go into detail about how companies can attract and retain the best people.

IF YOU ONLY REMEMBER ONE THING

A powerful, fulfilling and compelling vision from the leader will help a team set aside its individual differences and work together for a collective purpose.

CHAPTER 4

COMMUNICATION

WHAT IT'S ALL ABOUT ➡

- ▶ The difference between big talk and little talk
- ▶ The importance of integrity and consistency
- ▶ How to earn the right to be heard
- ▶ Why the stories people tell matter
- ▶ How to succeed in public speaking

A leader should never underestimate the impact their words (and actions) have on the people around them. The jobs, and future, of employees depend on decisions made by the leader, which means that employees will be listening closely to everything they say and watching everything they do. And yet many leaders consistently fail to give enough time or attention to the way in which they communicate.

There is little about being a good leader that has nothing to do with communication. Some would argue that communicating is just about *all* that leaders do. A leader can make the best strategic decisions in the world and the organisation could still fail if it was not communicated effectively – because how can people possibly reach a goal if they don't know where they are going, or how to get there?

The fact is that a single word, 'communication' covers an enormous range of leadership issues. A leader will spend every day communicating something to someone, in one form or another. This might mean communicating their vision for the team or organisation, as we discussed in Chapter 2, or communicating a change programme, as we will discuss in Chapter 7, or reassuring people during a crisis, which we will cover in Chapter 8. Or it might mean the everyday communication that is necessary to keep an organisation and its people motivated – and as we will see later, this may need a different approach for every individual. Or it might mean communicating with people outside of the business, such as customers, clients, suppliers or shareholders.

But this is not all. Everything the leader says, and everything they do, will have an effect on how they are perceived by their followers and by others as a leader. Every leader has a leadership 'brand', and every interaction they have, with people inside or outside of the organisation, will leave a trace on that brand. That brand is built on three elements: what leaders say, what they do, and what others say about them.

BIG TALK AND LITTLE TALK

Let's begin with the two connected but distinctive types of communication on which any business runs. Day-to-day leadership is, in effect, a combination of huge, fundamentally important decisions – such as setting the vision for the business, or implementing and seeing through a programme of change – and numerous, much smaller but everyday decisions and actions. The big decisions underpin a business, but it is the small, everyday actions that make sure that the big decisions are successfully followed through. This distinction between everyday communication and the communication of strategic priorities, was summarised by Martin Johnson, the former captain (and now coach) of the England rugby team as 'Big Talk' and 'Little Talk'. 'Little talk,' as he puts it, 'makes the big talk happen.'

The idea might have been identified on the rugby field, but it is equally relevant in the world of business. In a rugby context, the 'Big Talk' is the game plan and tactics that the team have discussed and rehearsed throughout their training. The 'Little Talk' is the conversation that goes on during the game, when players encourage each other, let each other know where they are, make necessary adjustments to the game plan to allow for pitch and weather conditions, and signal opportunities that other players might have missed. The team needs this constant communication during a game if they are to work together effectively as a group.

The 'Big Talk' in business is the leader's communication of where the business is heading. As we discussed in Chapter 2, leaders have to work extraordinarily hard to communicate the vision they have set to their followers. They must distil the vision down into simple concepts and repeat the message constantly, reinforcing it whenever they can and over every channel of communication. And the work of a leader does not end there. Leaders bear great responsibility for maintaining the motivational levels and morale of their team. On a 'Big Talk' level, this means constantly reminding everyone around them of the importance and value of what they are all doing and striving towards. It means keeping everyone informed of the worth of the goal, and of progress along the way.

'Little Talk' is essential in any environment. In a business environment it represents the everyday communication that underpins action, motivation and the overall confidence of the organisation. The leader's role is as essential as the conductor of an orchestra – through constant communication the leader keeps everyone together, on time and on track. If a leader remains largely silent and expects everyone around them to just get on with the job, the organisation will soon become directionless and demotivated. The importance of small words of encouragement applies equally to all leaders throughout an organisation – the absence of 'thank you', 'well done' and 'good job' is the single biggest sapper of motivational energy in a business.

This is not, incidentally, an invitation for all prospective leaders to drone on and on for hours about anything that might pop into their head. There is little point in talking if people are not listening to you, and the fastest way to guarantee an unresponsive audience is to talk too much and too often. If a leader has a specific message to get across they should expect to repeat themselves frequently, but never dilute the message with too much embellishment. Effective communication is carefully formulated and targeted – short, punchy and direct.

We should also make the point here that communication means nothing between a leader and followers unless the leader and their message is believed. A message might be heard, but that does not necessarily mean that it will be acted upon.

INTEGRITY AND CONSISTENCY

The personal impact that leaders have on followers – in other words, how followers *feel* about them when they see them – is a vital element of modern leadership. This phenomenon can clearly be seen during a political campaign, where it is not unusual for a candidate who inspires confidence and trust to win the communication war and come out on top, even if their policies are unclear (or even despicable). It's an extreme example, but the point is that a leader must have credibility. Irrespective of how often a leader repeats a message, it will not be accepted unless their followers believe in their leader.

WHO SAID IT

"A message is not necessarily accepted just because it is understood."
– John Kotter

As we discussed in Chapter 1, integrity is seen as an essential characteristic of a leader. The reason why becomes apparent when you think about how a leader persuades his (or her) followers to do what he (or she) says. Fear of reprisal is one option, of course, but one that was generally much more prevalent under the old approach to leadership that depended heavily on hierarchy and the power of authority. Modern-day leadership is more about persuasion and the power of earned respect. Generally people will do what their leader suggests because they think it's a good idea, or they see the benefits of doing it, or because they trust their leader to make the right decisions.

If people are going to listen to their leader, and follow them, the leader must have credibility. Once credibility is lost or damaged, followers lose trust in their leader, doubt the quality of their decision-making ability, and soon fall away. One of the best recent examples of this in business is the fall of Dick Fuld, the chairman and chief executive of Lehman Brothers. In 2007 he was named as one of the best CEOs in the world after overseeing a transformation in the investment company's fortunes and turning around a multi-million dollar loss to a profit of over $4 billion. But after initially being praised for coping well with the credit crisis, he was soon blamed for the collapse of Lehman Brothers after failing to accept an acquisition deal that could have saved it. In 2009 a US news channel named Fuld as its 'Worst American CEO of all time'.

The credibility of a leader depends mainly on the perception of their honesty and on the consistency of their words and their actions. Honesty can be a tricky concept, particularly in business and other situations where it might be tempting to keep the full truth from everyone around you. But most leaders argue that there are very few situations where honesty is not the best policy, mainly because people are more than capable of working out the truth for themselves. Military leaders are particularly firm on this point, and say that soldiers must always be given the full picture, even if the truth is less than palatable. If they are being asked to risk their lives it is essential that they trust their leaders and understand exactly what is being asked of them, and why.

A frequent mistake in business communication is that leaders omit the 'why'. Leaders spend much of their time explaining what needs to be done and when, but often forget to explain *why* it needs to be done. People need to understand the importance of what they are being asked to do, if they are to give their full commitment to the task. And when things go wrong, they need to understand why, to allay their fears that it will happen again.

CONSISTENCY IN ACTION

Followers are also looking for consistency from their leader, both in terms of the messages they communicate and in the sense that their actions and behaviour reinforce what they say, rather than contradict it. One of the most famous examples of a leader tripping over the consistency hurdle came in 1991, when Gerald Ratner, chief executive of the high street jewellery chain Ratner's, was asked to address the Institute of Directors' annual conference. Ratner peppered his speech with jokes and asides, one of them highlighting the range of products sold in his company's shops. As well as selling top-of-the range watches, he told the audience, his stores were also able to sell a set of sherry glasses on a silver tray for less than £10. And why? Because the set was 'crap'. The audience laughed on the day but journalists at the event picked up on the story and over the next few months, Ratner was accused of treating his customers with contempt and the company's stores became synonymous with poor-quality goods. The value of the company plunged and Ratner was fired a few months later. His commitment to the company, and love of it, was never in doubt but his ill-judged speech left the unfortunate impression that his pride in the company was somewhat superficial.

The actions of a leader must reflect what they say. There is little point in a leader asking their team to make more effort to go out and meet clients if the leader then spends all of their time in internal meetings.

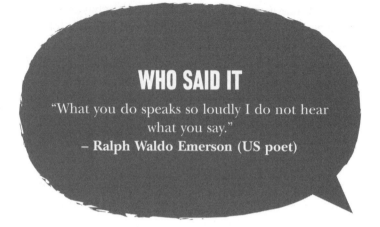

WHO SAID IT

"What you do speaks so loudly I do not hear what you say."
– Ralph Waldo Emerson (US poet)

So, a leader needs to be credible and to back up their words with their behaviour if they are to have the best chance of successfully getting their message across. But there is another vital element to communication that is often missed by leaders – and that is the rather under-rated practice of listening.

TWO-WAY COMMUNICATION

Many business leaders see communication as a one-way street and this view is often betrayed by the words they use to describe the process. Ask senior management to describe the communications strategy in their organisation and they will typically use language such as 'telling', 'informing', 'cascading' or 'briefing'. Similarly, if you were to try the 'T' test in many businesses, and ask a series of people at board and senior management level, as well as a line of employees through all levels of the business, what they thought of communication in their company, inevitably the senior managers would say it was excellent, but those further down the organisation would complain that it was poor and, crucially, that no-one ever listens to them.

While there are occasions where the best option is to tell someone what to do and make sure they do it, generally the best communication is two-way. There is a world of difference between information and communication, and between telling and sharing. Human beings thrive on interaction and crave conversation.

There are two important lessons here. The first is that two-way communication is the only way that a leader can stay in touch with reality. One of the biggest risks of leadership is that people will tell the leader what they think he or she wants to hear, rather than the truth. A leader can quickly become isolated from reality if they lose touch with what is really going on in the business.

EARN THE RIGHT TO BE HEARD

The second lesson is that a leader is far more likely to earn the trust, respect and loyalty of their followers if they listen to what their followers have to say. As we have seen, modern leadership is based on forming a relationship of mutual trust and respect between leader and follower, and that cannot happen if the leader does nothing but issue orders from above, without taking into account the opinions of people who are doing most of the work. It's relatively common to hear the complaint in business that a team is not listening to its manager – but that is usually because the manager is not listening to the team.

On a simple level, this means that the leader should be sure that they actively listen to the people around them. This may seem obvious, but how many of us can genuinely say that we listen well? Simon Woodroffe, the entrepreneur and founder of YO! Sushi, has deliberately developed a conversational habit which, on first meeting, is a little unsettling. If you speak to him or ask him question, there will be a lengthy pause before he answers. What he is doing is making sure that he listens to the entire question, before he begins to think about how he will answer. He does this because, after a few years in business he realised that he was beginning to formulate his response half way through the question – and that meant that he was not giving the questioner his full attention and in some cases was assuming that one question had been asked, when in reality it had been another. So Woodroffe now gives 100% of his attention to listening, then pauses to think, and then replies.

Followers like to know that they are heard, and that their opinions count. The best leaders create an environment where honest feedback is not only welcomed, but acted upon. The larger the group, however, the more difficult it is to carry out anything that could be described as a conversation and in large organisations, addressing everyone at once is simply not feasible. Good leaders employ a variety of techniques to get around this problem, such as addressing people in small groups so they have the opportunity to look each in the eye and to take questions.

The late Anita Roddick, founder of The Body Shop, came up with a novel solution to this conundrum. Every member of staff who joined the company was given an induction pack, which included a pack of scarlet red envelopes. The idea was that if you had a complaint or suggestion, or a good idea that could help to improve the business, you put it into a red envelope and sent it to the board of directors. Staff could send anonymous notes if they wanted to but if they signed their name, the board was obliged to respond to their comment within five days. The result was that staff knew that no comment would ever be ignored, and that their opinion counted.

Other business leaders have borrowed this idea in order to encourage a two-way conversation with staff, who might otherwise be too intimidated to ask a question, for example, during a group briefing with their leader. Turning communication into a conversation can be a challenge, but it brings dual benefits to a leader because it allows them to really understand what is going on in their team or business, and creates a vital sense of closeness between the leader and their followers.

CREATING CLOSENESS

A generation ago, it was perfectly acceptable for the leader of a business to work out of sight in a plush office, only appearing for an occasional rally of the troops or to tackle a crisis. These days, people want to see and hear their leader on a daily basis. Crucially, they also want to feel that they *know* their leader, which means treading a fine line between creating the distance that is necessary between leader and followers (necessary because, at some point, you might have to exert your authority or fire them), while creating a sense of closeness and intimacy.

WHO SAID IT

"The most important thing in communication is hearing what isn't being said."
– Peter Drucker (leadership writer)

Maintaining a sense of closeness is a challenge frequently faced by leaders as they move to higher levels of responsibility. The bigger the organisation, the more difficult it becomes to keep some sort of contact with everyone in the company. Add time pressure and the sheer volume of work expected of a CEO into the mix, and it's easy to see why some spend all their time in a palatial office at company headquarters, and why few of their employees could pick them out of a crowd.

This is why many leaders of large organisations go to great lengths to make themselves as visible as possible to everyone in the company. This might mean, for instance, making sure that their office is located at a hub of activity, where people from all levels of the organisation often walk by, or by having an office with glass walls so they can be seen by everyone (an option perhaps only for the brave), or by keeping their door open as much as possible. Sometimes the most efficient answer is to eat with everyone else in the staff canteen – a technique favoured by Charles Dunstone, co-founder of the Carphone Warehouse. 'You don't want to patronise people, but just try to be as much a normal member of the team as you can,' says Dunstone.

WHO YOU NEED TO KNOW
Greg Dyke

Dyke was director-general of the BBC between 2000 and 2004 and before that worked as a journalist and editor at London Weekend Television, TV-am and TVS. He was appointed by the BBC governors as the successor to John Birt and in terms of leadership style the two men were polar opposites. Birt was seen as an excellent administrator but distant and aloof, whereas Dyke's leadership style was based on forging an emotional bond with the BBC's employees.

When Dyke was appointed to the BBC he promised to 'cut the crap', and dismantle the internal market style of operations that Birt had championed. Dyke concentrated his efforts and more of the BBC resources on creative programme-making, where Birt had said that his aim was to make the organisation the best-run in the world. During Dyke's tenure the administrative costs at the BBC were reduced from 24% of its income to 15%. Dyke resigned from the organisation in the wake of the Hutton Inquiry, when he concluded that, as its leader, he had to bear ultimate responsibility for any failings by the BBC during the row over Andrew Gilligan's reporting on the run-up to the Iraq invasion, which accused the government of 'sexing up' its report on Saddam Hussein's weaponry.

Dyke has been widely studied as a leader, partly because his style is relatively unique and partly because he led the BBC through a time of fundamental and wide-ranging change. His views on winning the admiration and respect of his employees, and his techniques for communicating with a large number of people across multiple locations, are particularly valuable to aspiring leaders.

As well as remaining as visible as possible, good leaders always spare the time to speak to people individually whenever they can, even in the fast-paced modern world. Any leader will tell you that the question they hear more than any other is 'Have you got a minute?' When someone asks their leader for a minute, what they are really asking for is their undivided attention. The best leaders give it – if not straight away, then soon, and in a place where there will be no interruptions. It is a precious thing when someone gives you their close attention, particularly in this fast, modern world.

There is one other resource that good leaders use to create a sense of closeness with their followers, and to reinforce the air of credibility around them. However, this same resource can equally have a seriously damage effect on the image of a leader – it is the words of others.

THE STORIES PEOPLE TELL

It's not possible for a leader to be everywhere at once but in one sense, they always will be. Leaders are watched, judged and talked about every day. If they treat someone badly, word soon gets around but similarly, a good deed or impressive action will be retold and retold, inside and outside of the company.

The late MP and Northern Ireland Secretary Mo Mowlam, for instance, had an excellent reputation as someone who was able to connect with people from all walks of life. Her informal approach was legendary and a charac-teristic that set her apart from other politicians. That was undoubtedly her natural style, but some of her actions and habits served to reinforce that impression. For example, whenever Mowlam arrived at an office building she would follow the same course of action: greet the receptionist, introduce herself and ask her (or his) name.

Later, she would make a note of the name and building in her notebook. If she returned to the same office and a different receptionist was on duty, she did the same again, greet the receptionist, introduce herself and ask for her name. And when the receptionist gave her name Mowlam would then ask, by way of conversation, if it was the original receptionist's day off. It's a simple tactic, but the impact on staff at the business would be enormous – inevitably, the story would be told and retold that Mowlam took such an interest in the business that she even remembered the receptionists' names.

Greg Dyke quickly realised the power of the stories people tell about their leader while he was in charge of the BBC and its 10,000 employees. One morning, while heading from one meeting to another, he asked his regular BBC driver where he was planning to go for his holiday. The man said that he had booked a holiday abroad with his family, but that it had fallen through that morning because they had been double-booked by the holiday company. Dyke immediately offered the man use of his holiday home in Cornwall. By the end of the week, he said, the story had spread throughout the BBC.

The offer was a spur-of-the-moment one, but Dyke adds that he was not averse to making the occasional grand gesture while at the BBC, simply because he knew that the story would get around. One of his fundamental beliefs about leadership, for example, is that you get the best out of employees by supporting them, treating them well, and making it known that they are your immediate priority. He recounts an occasion when he was due to speak at a staff conference but the night before, his house was seriously damaged in a fire. 'I said I'd be there as soon as I could and I turned up at the conference looking a mess,' he says. 'The people at the conference would have gone back to their offices and said, guess what? His house burnt down and he still turned up. I suppose I could be quite calculated at times, in the things I did, but your people have to know that you put them first.'

MODERN COMMUNICATION

Modern communication innovations, such as email and social media, which were supposed to make business more efficient have, in fact, added to the pressure on leaders, simply because the volume of information they have to assess has increased exponentially, as has the speed of communication. Time management, as a result, has become a critical skill for all good business leaders and many have found a variety of ways of dealing with information and work overload.

Business leaders use a variety of techniques for managing email overload – Kevin Roberts, the worldwide CEO of Saatchi & Saatchi, for instance, does not check emails himself but asks his secretary to print out the messages that need a response, which he replies to by hand and which are then scanned and sent back to the sender.

Others set specific time aside to read emails during the day and do not check their inbox outside of those times, on the basis that constantly checking emails (or your BlackBerry) is an unwanted distraction from running the business.

There are many communication options for leaders in the modern world and it can be very tempting to fall back on email as a substitute for personal interaction, particularly when dealing with a larger group of followers. But leaders should approach any form of electronic communication with care because often what you gain on convenience and speed, you lose in the sense of personal closeness that is essential to modern leadership. The general rules is that any group communication such as emails should be interesting, snappy, as personal as possible, and – most importantly – have a point.

Mass email communication is particularly tricky in a larger business where people are spread over a number of sites, since it will inevitably mean that people read messages from their leader more frequently than they see them. A small number of business leaders in large organisations do successfully use email as a way of making sure that everyone feels involved and included, but this is a relatively rare skill. Done properly – and this generally means that emails are short, to the point and always entertaining – email can encourage workers, especially younger employees, to write back and provide valuable feedback.

Sir Richard Branson adopts this approach in his companies, writing his staff what he describes as 'chatty' letters and emails to let them know what is going on, and encouraging them to write back with comments and ideas. This is not an empty request – staff have his home address and telephone number, and every contact from staff receives a personal reply.

WHO YOU NEED TO KNOW
Sir Richard Branson

Richard Branson was born in 1950 and founded Virgin Records at the age of 22. His Virgin Group now consists of more than 350 companies and he is reputed to be worth more than £ 3 billion. Branson, a dyslexic, did not shine academically and left school at 16. He set up his first business, a magazine called *Student*, later that same year and in 1970 set up a record mail-order business, which he named 'Virgin' because most of his employees were new to business. Two years later he opened the first Virgin Records store in London and set up a record label, with Mike Oldfield's eventual best-seller *Tubular Bells* as its first release. Branson was a millionaire at the age of 25.

Branson's success as a businessman and leader has its roots in his ability to connect with people, and his willingness to take risks. His leadership style is often described as 'transformational', because of his informal style and lack of emphasis on hierarchy within his companies, and 'charismatic' because Branson and Virgin are so inextricably linked. Branson pays great attention to staff engagement and argues that all leaders hold a sense of moral responsibility to their employees. He believes strongly that you get the best out of people by treating them well, and with respect. During the recession of the early 1990s, he talked of how he tried, wherever possible, to move employees temporarily to a different part of the business, rather than make them redundant during difficult trading conditions, and said that this resulted in employee loyalty that was far more valuable than any short-term savings he could make by laying people off.

The same rules apply with electronic communication as with personal communication – good leaders try to encourage two-way communication and a sense of closeness with their followers. But email, along with other electronic forms of communication, such as intranets and webcasts, is essentially impersonal, even though it may be efficient in terms of time and effort in reaching many people at once. Used carefully and with skill, electronic communication can be effective but even those leaders that use it routinely and well, still take the time to talk to their people face-to-face whenever possible.

WHO SAID IT

"The single biggest problem in communication is the illusion that it has taken place."
– **George Bernard Shaw**

MANAGING MEETINGS

Meetings are an enormous potential waste of time for anyone in a leadership position, but again can be managed with some careful planning. Unfocused or unnecessary meetings no not only waste the leader's time – they disrupt the productivity of an organisation and can create an atmosphere where everything is done by consensus and the quality of work diminishes as a result. The best leaders set clear and solid rules around the meetings culture of their organisation, where everyone asks themselves before calling a meeting whether it is really necessary, what it is intended to achieve, and whether everyone on the list can contribute and so really needs to attend. It can be very helpful to carry out a regular 'meetings audit' of all the meetings that are held in an organisation and ask if they are all necessary, if some could be shorter, whether they are being held in a sensible place (in terms of travel time for everyone involved) and if some would be better held on a Friday afternoon rather than on a Monday morning.

The secret to a successful meeting is structure and time. Every meeting should have a clear purpose and the leader should have a strong idea of what should emerge at the end of it – a plan, an assignment of tasks, an idea, or so on. A clear agenda that is circulated to everyone beforehand will help to focus minds on what will be discussed (and avoiding 'any other business', which can be an excuse for a free-for-all, is usually advisable. A better option is to ask participants beforehand if there is anything else they want to add to the agenda). There should also be a set, and challenging, time limit to encourage everyone involved to remain focused on the key points.

Encouraging brevity in meetings is often a cultural challenge that has to be directly and specifically tackled by
leaders. One recruitment consultancy, for example spent
years beginning each week with an 8.15 am meeting on
Monday morning, at which team leaders would talk
about what they were planning to do that week, and any
developments that had come to light. Over time, these
weekly meetings – which were intended to last half an
hour – had stretched to 45 minutes, and then to an hour.
The leader's solution was to restrict everyone to two
minutes' speaking time, during which they had to summarise all of their points. Chaos reigned for two or three
weeks, when few people managed to get everything said
in the allotted time but within a month, the meeting was
back to 30 minutes, and stayed that way.

PUBLIC SPEAKING

It's impossible to avoid public speaking in some form
or another if you are a leader. But while public speaking
strikes terror into the heart of many people, the
good news is that effective presentation skills can be
learned.

Good presentation skills are a basic requirement for a
leader and, as with all skills, improve with constant practice. But again, preparation is an area that is often
neglected by leaders, partly because they may feel under

time pressure, and partly because leaders often underestimate the impact their words have on others. The words of the leader set the tone for the organisation and reassure everyone (if done correctly) that the business is on the right track and that the leader is in control. If the leader is hesitant, or less than fluid, or ill-prepared for questions, the result can be a damaging wave of uncertainty and insecurity that will be difficult to correct.

A 'big speech' – one that a leader makes in the wake of a change to the organisation, or in times of difficulty, will have far-reaching implications and should be given the priority it is due, and prepared thoroughly and meticulously. That said, it's always risky for a leader to speak to any group on any occasion without some preparation – very few people are able to convey the message they want to off the cuff. The safest option is to have a few 'standard' speeches to hand, containing your key messages – such as underlining the vision for the business – that can be adapted to any situation.

The temptation when writing a speech or presentation is to think first about content, and then about structure. But the first question for a leader should be: What do I want my audience to think, feel or do? Do you want them to be reassured? Enthused and motivated? Involved? Clear about a target or direction?

A good speech will have a macro message and a series of micro messages and stories that support the overall objective. Television news journalists use a similar technique when covering a major or complicated story. Take, for example, the coverage of the Tsunami in South-East Asia in 2004. With a disaster on that scale, with hundreds of thousands killed and millions killed or displaced, the challenge for journalists was how to convey the personal impact of a tragedy that had killed so many and covered such a wide area. So, the news reports began with an explanation of what a Tsunami was and how it was triggered, followed by a map of South-East Asia, showing the location of the original earthquake and where the waves had struck shore. And in order to engage the audience with the significance of the tragedy – the sheer scale of the numbers of victims is a difficult concept for anyone to fully grasp – the reports would then concentrate on a fisherman from the east coast of Sri Lanka who had lost his sons, his wife, his home and his fishing boat. The juxtaposition of the 'big story' facts and stories illustrating the personal-level tragedy of the event are an extremely effective way of getting the full message across. People remember stories far better than facts.

On either side of the main messages, good speeches begin with an attention grabber – a bold statement, surprising statistic, or a question, rather than a list of housekeeping points or pleasantries – and finish with a series of short but strong sentences which summarise rather than repeat the main points. Repetition and alliteration add impact and help the audience remember key points and messages, and while they may look out of place on the page, work well when spoken.

DELIVERING A SPEECH

Even experienced leaders suffer from nerves, but recognise that nerves are useful in getting adrenaline moving around the body. The best antidote to nerves is to be as well-prepared as possible – which means setting aside time before hand:

▶ Write out your presentation in full, bearing in mind that the written and spoken word is not the same thing. We tend to speak in short sentences, so edit and add punctuation as you go.

▶ Learn the speech. The most efficient way is to read it aloud and record yourself, and then listen to it over and over (car journeys are particularly useful for this) until it sinks in.

▶ Remember you don't have to be word perfect – in fact, you will sound more natural if you are not. But learn the first two minutes word-for-word – that is when you will feel the most nervous.

▶ Make notes onto small cards if you think you may need a prompt.

▶ If you are speaking away from the office, visit the venue before the event and spend some time getting familiar with the environment. Remove any surprises from the equation: How does the audio system sound? Will you be able to see the audience with the lights on? If you are using Powerpoint or an audio/visual system,

> how does it work? If you are taking questions, who will have microphones for the audience?
> ▶ Check and double-check audio visual equipment, and have a contingency if things go wrong.

Effective public speaking does take some practice, but obeying some basic rules will start you off on the right track:

- ▶ Never begin until there is complete silence in the room, even if that means waiting.
- ▶ Divide the audience into sections and look at each in turn, making eye contact if possible.
- ▶ Vary your pitch, volume and pace. Don't be afraid of dramatic pauses and emphasise key words.
- ▶ Move away from the lectern if you can and use your movements to emphasise your points.
- ▶ If you are using Powerpoint, talk to the audience and not to the screen. Keep the content limited to a maximum of six lines per slide, and don't use more than one slide every three minutes. If you want to give more detail, use handouts.

Speaking in public is the most exposed form of communication that a leader will do, but even then it is not what they say that is important, but how they say it. The American psychologist Albert Mehrabian says in his book *Silent Messages* that when someone is talking about their feelings or attitudes, the listener will make a judgment that is based 55% on the speaker's appearance and body language, 38% the tone of their voice and 7% on what they actually say. Mehrabian argues that if communication is to be effective and meaningful, these three elements of the message need to harmonise. Mehrabian was not necessarily speaking of a business context but it is an important message for business leaders in the modern world – what they say is only part of what makes them a leader.

Communication makes up an enormous part of a leader's role but as we have seen, it is far more than simply sending out key messages and expecting them to be heard and acted upon. It's true to say that modern technology, rather than making communication easier for leaders, has complicated the issue somewhat by creating a lot more noise over which they must be heard. Perhaps this is one reason why modern leaders must be more engaging than their predecessors – after all, anyone can talk, but who will listen?

WHAT YOU NEED TO READ

▶ There are numerous books available on communication, offering a range of thoughts and advice for potential leaders. *Great Communication Secrets of Great Leaders* (McGraw

Hill, 2003) by John Baldoni is one of the better ones. *The Leader's Voice* by Boyd Clarke and Ron Crossland (Select Books, 2004) is also worth a look.

▶ For real-life examples of good communicators in action, try Greg Dyke's *Inside Story* (Harper Collins, 2004) and Richard Branson's *Screw it, Let's Do It* (Virgin Books, 2006).

▶ Carmine Gallo is an American consultant who specialises in business communication and his website, www.carminegallo.com contains some useful tips. He has also written a number of books which study the actions and behaviour of current business leaders, including *The Presentation Secrets of Steve Jobs.* And for tips on what works in a speech, try *Insights and Lessons From 100 of the Greatest Speeches Ever Delivered* by Simon Maier and Jeremy Kourdi (Marshall Cavendish, 2010).

▶ For some invaluable tips on how to make the most of your speaking voice from an expert in the subject, look no further than *Your Voice and How To Use It* (Virgin Books, 1994) by the theatrical voice coach Cecily Berry.

IF YOU ONLY REMEMBER ONE THING

There is much more to communication than speaking. Everything a leader does, as well as everything they say, sends a message to followers.

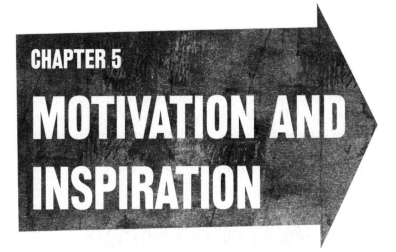

CHAPTER 5
MOTIVATION AND INSPIRATION

WHAT IT'S ALL ABOUT ➡

- ▶ How to motivate without money
- ▶ The ingredients of motivation
- ▶ Inspirational leaders
- ▶ Ways of keeping everyone involved
- ▶ A desire to impress is a strong motivator

A leader can make the most tactically brilliant decisions but it will mean nothing unless he or she can persuade everyone around them to commit all of their energy and ability into making the decision happen. Motivating followers is a difficult challenge for many leaders, sometimes because motivating people does not come naturally to them, but often because sustaining a level of motivation can be an utterly exhausting exercise.

MONEY DOESN'T MOTIVATE

Before we start on motivational techniques, let's start by exploding a myth. One of the most common mistakes made in business – and certainly the most widespread – is the assumption that money motivates people to perform at their best. This is simply not true – at least, not in the vast majority of circumstances.

The belief that the more you pay people, the more effort they will offer has been around for a long time. It still is – the business world runs on bonuses, commissions and other incentives. For a while, it worked. But not today. So what has changed? As the management writer and journalist Daniel Pink explains so convincingly in his book *Drive*, what has changed is the nature of work. Pink points out that successive and compelling studies by experts in psychology and human behaviour have shown beyond doubt that paying people more to complete a task only works when the task has a simple set of rules and an obvious outcome. So, for example, if you tell a group of workers to produce 100 identical widgets in as quick a time as possible, and that there will be a reward for those who complete the task fastest, monetary reward works a treat. They all understand what they have to do and that if they do it quicker than anyone else, they get more money.

Monetary incentives are, in other words, awfully good at focusing people on a mechanical straightforward task. The problem is that business life is not so simple. Very few tasks involve straightforward tasks with a beginning and an end. Business typically involves making complex decisions, creativity and innovation, and the same studies have shown that if you offer someone a monetary reward to carry out these types of tasks more quickly, or better, than anyone else they will almost certainly fail.

WHO SAID IT

"Crisis is the greatest motivator in the world."
– **Ursula Burns (CEO Xerox)**

Instead, Pink argues that people at work in the modern world are motivated by three things, which he terms 'autonomy, mastery and purpose'. In other words, we are all motivated by the human desire to be in control of our own lives, to keep learning and to excel at something, and to feel that we are working towards a higher purpose.

You will hear many variations of this central idea. The management writer John Kotter, for example, put it well when he said that motivation and inspiration energise people, not by pushing them in the right direction as you might do under a control and command leadership style, but by satisfying some basic human needs, by which he meant our need for achievement, recognition, self-esteem, the need to have some control over our own lives, and the chance to live up to our ideals. 'Such feelings touch us deeply,' said Kotter, 'and elicit a powerful response.'

If you read the views of a selection of leaders and leadership writers and academics, the ingredients of motivation will vary slightly but, in essence, they all circle around similar the three elements that Daniel Pink identified. Mutual trust and respect, interesting work and achievable goals are ideas that frequently crop up. The generally accepted view is that employees will be motivated to do their best if: they believe in the vision, direction or objectives of the task or organisation; they feel that they well-informed, have the resources they need, and are trusted to do their job; they have a challenging but achievable target; and they feel that the company cares for their welfare.

INSPIRATIONAL LEADERS

The best modern leaders – and those who practice the authentic and empathetic style of leadership that we talked about in Chapter 1 – already understand that they need to appeal to basic human needs in order to get the best out of their people. Sometimes these leaders are called 'inspirational' leaders because of their ability to make people feel that they can be the best possible versions of themselves. In effect, what these leaders are doing is fulfilling the basic needs of autonomy, mastery and purpose (albeit particularly well).

Motivation and inspiration are not the same thing, incidentally, but they have a very similar effect. The dictionary definition of motivation is 'the act of giving somebody a reason or incentive to do something', whereas inspiration is 'a force or influence on people' to stimulate creativity, ideas or moral fervour. The definitions are interesting in that one (the definition of motivation) seems easier to grasp than the other, because motivation is more based in reality and solid fact (give a reason to someone for doing something, and they will do it), whereas inspiration is more ethereal and difficult to pin down. And it is equally true to say that while techniques can be learned that create a motivational atmosphere in an organisation, genuinely inspirational leaders tend to be born rather than made.

While these three basic ingredients work well on a general level, on an individual level, no two people are motivated by the same thing and it's up to the leader to work out what works best for each. One might need encouragement and praise; another might need nothing more than a clear target in order to produce their best work. Some are motivated by a need to impress others, or to prove themselves better than them; others are driven by a fear of failure. Working out what motivates an individual depends on the leader's ability to read and understand people, which is why modern leadership requires emotional intelligence.

PURPOSE

Let's look at the three elements identified by Daniel Pink more closely, starting with purpose – the need to feel that we are achieving something great. The feeling of purpose, or is closely linked to the vision of the organisation, which will have been set by the leader. A clear vision, which sets out a target that is achievable but challenging, and is one that people can see the benefit of reaching, is a strong motivating factor in itself.

The best business leaders tend to place an emphasis on connecting people to a bigger picture. This means that everyone in the company, whether they work in accounts or IT or sales or on the reception desk, know that their work contributes to the ultimate success of the business and to the 'vision' of the leader. But some leaders go still further than that – they don't concentrate entirely on the plan or achievements of the organisation, but on what that might mean to the world at large. In other words, they tell their people that their work matters, and that it has a wider purpose. As Kevin Roberts, the worldwide CEO of the advertising agency Saatchi & Saatchi says, 'the role of a leader is to share a dream. We all want to work for something bigger than a pay cheque and bigger than producing a new laundry detergent' – the role of the leader is to show people that their work has a meaning that goes beyond the tasks they perform every day.

Saatchi & Saatchi is a highly creative, ideas-driven business that has a very young and highly mobile workforce – the average age of its employees is 27 and 20% of its staff leave every year to move on to other opportunities (although some return to Saatchi later). The high rate of staff turnover is not a symptom of an unhappy organisation, but an indication that it tends to attract creative and restless people who are more likely to want to explore a variety of experiences, such as living in a different country, or setting up their own business. And this is something that Roberts embraces, rather than tries to 'fix'. He reasons that while his parents' generation did not expect to get much enjoyment out of their jobs and so were not disappointed when they didn't get it, the latest generation (usually referred to in business as

Generation Y – those born after 1980) are different. They are looking for and expect fulfilment and enjoyment out of their work. 'These kids are not going to stay with a company for five minutes if they're not loving it,' says Roberts.

WHO YOU NEED TO KNOW
Kevin Roberts

The worldwide chief executive of the advertising agency Saatchi & Saatchi was born in relative poverty in Lancaster and credits the deputy head of his local comprehensive school with helping to turn his life around after he was expelled from grammar school at the age of 17. He began his career as brand director to the designer Mary Quant in London in the 1960s before moving on to Gillette, Procter & Gamble and Pepsi Cola.

He was appointed worldwide CEO of Saatchi & Saatchi in 1997, at a time when the group was struggling with poor performance and low morale. It is said that Roberts was advised when he joined the company to restructure the business and bring in new and fresh talent from outside the organisation. Instead, he kept everyone in their current role and within a year, the company was beginning to recover.

Roberts has a distinctive style, both in terms of fashion (he is always in black and never wears a tie) and leadership. He was one of the first CEOs of a large organisation to actively practice empathetic leadership and strongly believes that his role is to hire the right people, to give them what they need, make sure they are happy, and let them get on with their work with the minimum of intervention.

AUTONOMY AND MASTERY

Daniel Pink's other two ingredients for motivating people are autonomy – our basic human need to control our own lives – and mastery – our need to be good at what we do. Again, these elements can be seen in the behaviour of good business leaders. They tend to tell their followers that anything is possible, and help them to believe in themselves. They work hard at improving confidence and self-belief by constantly praising achievement, by concentrating on the strengths of people rather than on their weaknesses, and by giving their people the resources they need to do their job, and largely leaving them alone to do it. They believe that, by leaving people to work out problems for themselves rather than by looking over their shoulder and telling them what to do, their confidence will flourish. There are risks in this approach, of course, but the best leaders are willing to accept them for the sake of results.

As part of this approach, these leaders make a concerted effort to really listen to the people within their business – and this does not mean playing lip service to feedback, but actively creating systems and forums where ideas are encouraged, welcomed and, if they work, quickly acted upon. People either see their ideas come to fruition, or clearly understand why they are not. Kevin Roberts argues that involving staff in everything he does, including setting the vision for the business, means that they are more committed to the outcome.

A number of companies actively embrace the idea of autonomy, sometimes with spectacular results. Google, for instance, runs an initiative that it calls '20% time', which sets employees free to work on any project of their own that they like, as long as it is not connected to their everyday work, for one day a week. Some of the company's most innovative ideas – including gmail – have come out of this process.

THE POWER OF MORALE

Let's take a moment to talk about the power of motivation. Business is not war (whatever some people may tell you), but business leaders can learn a great deal from the approach of their counterparts in the armed forces. Military training focuses heavily on leadership skills and some of the most effective leaders, in terms of inspiring and motivating their followers to achieve what may seem impossible at the outset, come from the armed forces. When you think about what the leaders of soldiers, sailors and airmen have to do – persuade them to risk their lives in the course of doing what their leaders ask – it is clear that the military has lessons to teach us all about the power of motivation.

Military leaders talk of the morale of their men, rather than of motivation, but the two are closely linked. Morale is defined as 'the mental attitude or bearing of an individual or group, especially as regards confidence and discipline'. High morale is essential if an army is going to function to the best of its ability – Lord Inge, the former chief of staff, says that without it, an army is nothing but a collection of frightened, unhappy men. Famous battles throughout history, from Agincourt to the Battle of Britain, show that a smaller group of fighters can beat their opponents even when vastly outnumbered, provided their morale is high – as though the collective sense of self-belief creates a collective power that is far greater than the sum of the individuals involved. As a result, military leaders work hard to maintain morale at all times.

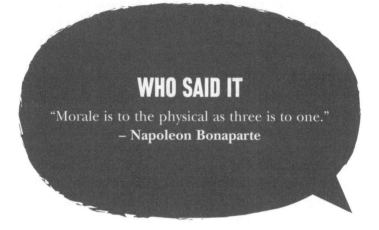

WHO SAID IT

"Morale is to the physical as three is to one."
– Napoleon Bonaparte

Viscount Slim, who fought in both the first and second World Wars, once said that morale has to have strong mental, spiritual and material foundations. In other words, the soldiers need to believe that what they are doing is important, that the aims are achievable and that they are as well-prepared and armed as they could possibly be. The best military leaders spend a lot of time and effort making sure that these needs are fulfilled, and actively demonstrating to their men that they have all the support that they need.

Major General Patrick Cordingley, who commanded the Desert Rats during the first Gulf war, says that while stationed with his men in the Saudi Arabian desert awaiting the order to advance into Kuwait, he made sure that the men repeatedly rehearsed the evacuation procedure for injured soldiers – not because they needed to practice, but because it helped to reassure the men that if they were injured, everything possible would be done to get them to help as quickly as possible. By the end of the exercise, all of his men knew that an injured solider would reach a field hospital within an hour and a half. This consistent reinforcement of the view that the leader has the best interests of their followers in mind is vital to maintaining morale, and is equally relevant in the business world. People need to know that their leader, and the business, will look after them and support them. If the company gives its best to them, they will give their best to the company.

MOTIVATION IN PRACTICE

If you know what to look for, it is possible to see business leaders putting motivational theory into practice. An excellent example is Sir Terry Leahy, the recently-retired chief executive of Tesco, who has said that the success of a leader depends on maintaining a happy workforce. He argued that a leader must provide four basic things in order to satisfy and motivate their people: an interesting job; the chance to improve their prospects; respect; and a boss who helps them, rather than being their biggest problem.

Tesco is an interesting example of the difficulties facing many leaders in motivating workers, simply because of the sheer size of its workforce (472,000 at the last count), the majority of which are in relatively low-paid jobs. The success of the business depends to a large extent, as Sir Terry has said repeatedly, on the work and attitude of its checkout assistants and shelf stackers. And, he argued, how these people do depends not on the targets that are set for them or the rules they have to abide by, but on how they feel about their employer.

With this in mind, Tesco has developed a very distinct management style. First of all, it spends a lot of time encouraging its people. 'Retailing is a tough, competitive environment,' is how Sir Terry puts it, 'but we spend most of our time making people feel good about themselves and the job they do. They don't go around with criticism ringing in their ears. We consciously build confidence and motivation.' Second, it has made sure that progress through the organisation is not only possible, but the norm. There are very few demarcation lines between the various jobs in the company so, within reason, most of the people who work for the company could do any job. The roles are not consciously separated and employees do not feel that they are stuck in a rut by the company's structure.

Third, the hierarchical structure of the company reinforces an atmosphere of possibility. There are only six management levels between a checkout assistant and the CEO, and at any one time one in ten of Tesco's staff are in training for the next level. The clear message is that if you are prepared to put the work in, progress is achievable.

Fourth, many of the employees have a vested interest in the success of the business. Of its 472,000 employees worldwide, 195,000 have a personal stake in the business through its share scheme.

And finally, Sir Terry as a leader consistently backed up the company's approach in his own behaviour. For one week every year, for example, he worked as a shelf stacker in one of the stores. Doing so served two purposes – it gave him a first-hand view of any of the problems that front-line workers were facing, but it also reinforced the statement that anything was possible. If he could do a shelf stacker's job then, in theory, a shelf stacker could do his.

WHO YOU NEED TO KNOW
Sir Terry Leahy

The chief executive of the UK's largest supermarket group, Sir Terry Leahy is often held up as an example of outstanding leadership, credited with Tesco's enormous expansion as a retailer domestically and internationally, and its movement into new market.

Leahy was born in Liverpool and educated at the local grammar school, and during the school holidays travelled to London to work in Tesco's Wandsworth branch as a shelf-stacker because he couldn't find work closer to home. After completing a degree in management sciences in UMIST Leahy applied to joined Tesco, as part of its graduate traning programme, but the job was offered to another candidate. Two years later in 1979, Leahy applied again and joined the company as a marketing executive.

He was appointed to the board in 1992, three years before the company became the UK's largest retailer, and succeeded his mentor, Lord MacLaurin, as chief executive in 1997. Much of Leahy's success at Tesco has been attributed to his strategy of concentrating on understanding his customers' behaviour better, rather than simply following the trends of other retailers. One of his greatest successes was the introduction of the Clubcard loyalty scheme which, as well as encouraging repeat purchases, enabled the company to monitor the buying habits of its customers. While Leahy has attracted criticism for making Tesco 'too large', he continued with his aggressive expansion strategy before announcing his intention to retire in March 2011.

Tesco is an excellent example of the challenges of motivating a large group of people, and brings us to another key behavioural technique of good leaders – they make a concerted effort to make sure that everyone feels involved in the success of the business.

CELEBRATING SUCCESS, COLLECTIVELY

Celebrating successes, even small ones, is a vital element in maintaining motivation. It appeals to the basic human need to be recognised for our efforts, and allows the leader to demonstrate clearly that something is being achieved. Celebrating success is also vital because it concentrates everyone's mind on what went right. It's often the case in business that too much time is spent on analysing what went wrong in any particular situation, while too little time is spent in analysing what went right. After all, it's the successes rather than the failures that businesses and their leaders want to emulate. If you don't understand why you won, how can you hope to repeat it?

Good leaders take the time to pause and celebrate with their followers when something has gone well. Greg Dyke says he understood the importance of small celebrations after visiting a US company, where he saw that a room had been set aside to store presents – it was full of balloons, plants and other small gifts. He was told that anyone in the company could choose a present and send it to a colleague as a 'thank you', if they had helped them with something or if they felt they deserved a reward. 'I thought that was really clever because it cost the business peanuts in terms of money,' says Dyke, 'but can you imagine the reaction if you're sitting at your desks and someone comes along with a present for you?'

While he was director-general of the BBC, Dyke says he frequently took the time to write a short email to employees congratulating them on a particularly good programme. He sent one to everyone in the organisation the day after the BBC broadcast the Queen's Jubilee concert, during which the guitarist Brian May played on the roof of Buckingham Palace. 'I came into the office the next day and send and email to everyone, just saying, 'Wasn't that wonderful? Didn't we do well?' Everyone might have felt that at the time, but it was important to say it.'

It's important to note here that Greg Dyke sent his congratulatory email to everyone in the BBC, whether they were directly involved in the broadcasting of the concert or not. That is because he was careful to treat every success as a group effort – which is vital in maintaining the collective motivation of an organisation.

COLLECTIVE INVOLVEMENT

Inevitably – and this is particularly true of large organisations – some people in a company will be more directly involved in the achievement of a goal than others. Some will feel very involved and will be there at the point of success (or failure). Others will have played a vital support role which means that achievement could not have happened without them, and yet they will feel detached – which is a problem for the leader because people who are detached from results tend to become demotivated quite quickly. But the situation could quickly become more serious than that, if those employees who are not directly involved in a success begin to feel resentment that their contribution is being ignored or forgotten.

Good leaders understand the importance of involving everyone in their pursuit of a vision. There is a frequently repeated account of a visit that the US President John F. Kennedy made to NASA's Space Center in 1962. As he was heading along a corridor the President stopped to talk to one of the employees, a janitor. 'Hello,' said the President, 'and what do you do here?' The janitor replied: 'Mr President, I'm helping to put a man on the moon.'

It may not be true but it's still a great story because it neatly illustrates that you don't have to be at the action end of a business to feel motivated by the common purpose of the organisation. But the fact that NASA's janitor did feel that he was contributing to the end goal is a tribute to its strength of leadership – because that sense of involvement must be created and nurtured by the leader.

Ron Dennis, the former chief executive of the Formula One racing team McLaren, was another leader who made a real effort to make sure that everyone in his company felt as involved as possible in its successes. The nature of Formula One means that there are a relatively small team of McLaren workers who travel around the world, from one race to the next. They work on refining the cars and supporting the drivers, and they are at the track for each race. If a McLaren car wins, they are all there to celebrate, first hand, as a team. But the remaining 200 or so McLaren employees watch the race at home on television, with the rest of the worldwide audience. In the busy excitement of the Formula One season it would be easy to forget the people left at home, but Dennis understood the importance of making sure that all of his employees knew that he recognised the role that each one played in each race, from the receptionist to the team drivers.

After each race the Ron Dennis returned to the company headquarters in Surrey and collected all of the employees together in the staff canteen. It's a room that can hold maybe 120 seated diners but after race day more than 200 people crammed into the canteen, crowded into every corner and some standing on tables. Dennis talked through the race to them in every detail, explaining what happened at every stage and the decisions the team made behind the scenes. By the end of the session everyone in the company knew the story of the race from the racing team's point of view. Dennis described this as the 'insider feeling' – making sure that everyone felt part of a team, felt included and knew that their contribution, whatever it was, was appreciated.

WHO SAID IT

"I don't want to hear that the person sitting on reception has any less responsibility here than the Director of Operations. In fact, it is the person sitting on reception who will probably field the phone calls from the President of the International Olympics Committee. Everyone is in this together."

– Lord Coe

LOYALTY AND AFFECTION

One of the strongest motivational compulsions is a follower's desire to impress their leader. Some of the most successful organisations in recent years have been led by people who command not only the respect, but also the loyalty and the affection, of their followers.

Greg Dyke undoubtedly earned the affection and loyalty of his employees while at the BBC, which could be clearly seen when thousands of them demonstrated outside their offices on the day that he resigned. Some of this affection was formed by the simple fact that the organisation became more successful during his leadership, but most came down to his ability to empathise with his employees. Many modern business leaders argue that a sense of empathy is essential in motivating employees, saying that it forms the basis of the difference of a leader ordering their people to head over a hill and them saying, 'I'm going over that hill' and the followers replying, 'OK, we're coming with you'.

Dyke fostered this sense of empathy through his habit of communicating in a personal style, by asking everyone to call him Greg, by making sure he replied to anyone who wrote to him, and by writing personal notes to any employee who was suffering a tragedy or experiencing something joyful. Dyke argues that all of us have up to 10 'significant days' in our lives, which might be our wedding day, or the day our children or grandchildren are born, or the day our parents or another loved-one die. Dyke believes that it is only right for a leader to mark and acknowledge each of those significant days for anyone who works for them – by sending them a personal letter of condolence, or flowers, or by celebrating with them. Dyke argues that this is just the human thing to do, but the end result is that people feel that they are being treated as real people with real lives, and not just as employees.

Those leaders who inspire the most affection among their employees tend to be those that create an atmosphere of personal closeness between leader and follower. Good military leaders are especially talented at this, which is surprising considering that the armed forces operate under a strict hierarchy. The best military leaders inspired a level of devotion among their men, which meant that they would follow the leader anywhere, without question. It is usually the case that this devotion was nurtured by the leader's repeated demonstration that he put the welfare of the men above all – when Admiral Nelson was hit by shrapnel during one battle, for instance, the ship's surgeon was called away from a wounded man to help, but Nelson waved him away, saying that he would take his turn 'alongside my brave men'. Military leaders repeatedly talk of the importance of demonstrating to their men that their welfare is the leader's first consideration – by, for example, ordering that the men's quarters be set up in a new camp before the officers' mess.

WHO SAID IT

"I've always felt that a manager has achieved a great deal when he's able to motivate one other person. When it comes to making a place run, motivation is everything."
– **Lee Iacocca (former CEO Chrysler)**

CLOSE, BUT NOT TOO CLOSE

The important proviso here is that the relationship between leader and follower may be close – or appear to be close – but it is one based on personal respect and affection, rather than on some of the qualities that underpin friendships in our personal lives. Part of the horror of David Brent's leadership style in *The Office* was his undying belief that he had to be his employees' friend, and that it was up to him to make work 'fun'. Many inspirational leaders – and others – talk of the importance of having fun at work. What they mean is that people should enjoy their work and be stimulated by it, rather than any suggestion of David Brent-inspired joshing and practical jokes. Forcing people to have 'fun' is unlikely to work as a motivational tool – in fact, it's more likely to annoy them. 'Fun' should be an organic by-product of a stimulating and motivating job.

Leadership is not a friendship contest. There are real benefits to a leader being close to their followers, because it allows the leader to learn about their followers, which is a basic requirement to managing them well, and because it allows the followers to know more of the leader, which (ideally) encourages loyalty, trust and commitment. But it's difficult, and some would say impossible, for a leader to have a genuine friendship with any of their followers.

Motivation is a complex subject and we will return to it again, in a different guise, when we talk about how leaders manage performance and encourage high performance. The thought that it is up to you, as a leader, to act as the fuel that fires the motivational power of the business can be an intimidating idea but the elements discussed in this chapter should help to form a solid platform on which to build. It's true to say that many leaders manage to be highly motivational without thinking about it too much, since their enthusiasm for the business they're in or team they lead does much of the work for itself.

WHAT YOU NEED TO READ

▶ Daniel Pink's book on motivation, *Drive: The Surprising Truth About What Motivates Us* (Riverheard, 2009), is a fascinating read and more information can be seen on the author's website, *www.danpink.com*. Also worth reading is John Adair's *Leadership and Motivation: The Fifty-Fifty Rule and the Eight Key Principles of Motivating Others* (Kogan Page, 2009), which contains useful tips to put into practice.

▶ One of the best ways to learn about motivation and the way leader inspire people to do their best is to read the accounts of leaders in different situations. Lee Iacocca, the CEO of Chrysler between 1978 and 1992, produced an interesting *Autobiography* (Sedgewick & Jackson, 1985), which details how he worked to turn around the struggling company. Kevin Roberts of Saatchi & Saatchi writes a regular blog, www.krconnect.blogspot.com, which often discusses his views on motivating and inspiring people. Kevin's website (www .saatchikevin.com) is also worth a look.

▶ Alexander Kjerulf calls himself a 'chief happiness officer' and has some interesting things to say on happiness at work and how it relates to employee motivation (www.positivesharing .com).

IF YOU ONLY REMEMBER ONE THING

People tend to be motivated by basic human emotions, rather than by monetary reward.

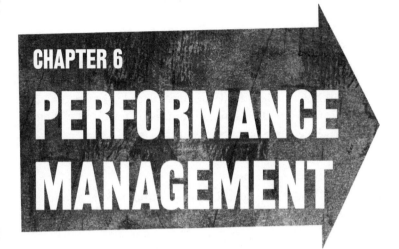

CHAPTER 6

PERFORMANCE MANAGEMENT

WHAT IT'S ALL ABOUT ➤

- ▶ The meaning of high performance
- ▶ Ways of setting targets and measuring performance
- ▶ How to assess your team
- ▶ Ways of dealing with high, developing and poor performers
- ▶ How to develop the next generation of leaders

A team or business is only as good as its people. Successful companies are built on the back of the performance of their employees and in the previous chapters we talked about how leaders find the best people, and work to motivate them. The ultimate aim is to encourage them to produce their best, consistently.

In the leadership world, this is often talked about as encouraging 'high performance'. But what do we mean by high performance? What drives some people perform to the absolute limit of their ability, while others are content to coast, or to do a task well, without stretching themselves to do it better?

High performance, and particularly how leaders can encourage and develop high performance in their followers, is an area that has attracted a lot of interest in the study of leadership. Interest in the subject is invariably stronger during a recession, when companies are forced to cut back on their workforce and must instead concentrate on coaxing greater levels of productivity out of a smaller group of employees. But high performance should be a constant concern for anyone who wants to be a good (or great) leader, and not just something they think about during a crisis. The best leaders are those that have the ability to encourage everyone to do their absolute best, all of the time.

WHO SAID IT

"A man should never be appointed to a
managerial position if his vision focuses on
people's weaknesses rather than on
their strengths."
– **Peter Drucker**

Managing performance (which is generally taken to
mean managing under-performance rather than stimulating high performance) is a relatively new concept in
terms of the study of leadership, which is curious considering that no leader can be effective if they are incapable
of encouraging people to perform at their best. The
writer and consultant Peter Drucker was relatively
unusual among the well-known names in leadership, in
that he argued through most of his life that the value of
a business was built on its people, and that the main role
of a leader (or manager, as he termed it) was to bring
out the best in their people. Drucker argued consistently
that leaders should look for the strengths in their people,
and find ways of improving their talents and applying
their abilities in the most effective way for the company.

WHO YOU NEED TO KNOW
– Peter Drucker

Born in Austria in 1909 (he died in 2005), Peter Drucker began his career as a journalist in Germany before leaving the country in 1933 for England, and later the US, where he became a naturalised citizen and lectured at New York University. He later developed the US' first MBA programme at Claremont Graduate School.

Drucker's particular area of interest was the behaviour of humans and the way they develop and manage relationships with each other. He studied what he called 'social ecology' in a variety of contexts, including the business world. Drucker believed strongly that people are a company's most valuable resource and that the role of a leader was to give them the freedom and power to perform. He consistently spoke against the 'command and control' model of leadership and felt that an organisation could only produce its best if it was decentralised. One of his best-known arguments was the importance of creating a 'community' in all parts of our lives, but particularly at work, because humans are essentially social animals. In his later years, though, he became disillusioned with the way many companies were run and in the 1980s condemned the growing trend of high pay for executives, arguing that a CEO should not be paid more than 20 times the rate of a rank and file worker. He later began to express doubts about the ability of a corporation to create a supportive community, and became an outspoken critic of capitalism.

Drucker's first book was *Concept of the Corporation*, the result of a two-year study into the workings of General Electric in the 1940s. He wrote 39 books in total, including *The Practice of Management* and *The Effective Executive.*

But how can does a leader know when someone is performing at their best, and how can they encourage high performance from a diverse group of people? To understand the process, you first have to understand what makes people perform to the limit of their ability.

WHAT IS HIGH PERFORMANCE?

Some of the most interesting research around high performance in recent years has been carried out by an Australian, Andrew Meikle, who until the late 1990s was a regular competitor in Australia's Iron Man surf-lifesaving series. The events – a series of exhausting and potentially crippling marathon challenges involving board paddling, swimming, ski paddling and running – were fought over by 30 of the country's most élite (and arguably certifiably insane) athletes. Over the course of a number of seasons, Meikle became obsessed with understanding why he was consistently failing to break into the top five finishers. He always finished well – usually in the top ten – but what, he wondered, was setting the top three and five apart from the rest? Were they just better athletes? Or was there something in their psyche and attitude that made them better than anyone else?

As a result of his research into high-performers in just about every part of life, Meikle was able to identify a set of circumstances that seem to trigger improved performance in human beings, some of which are drawn on in this chapter. At the root of his conclusion, though, is the existence of healthy competition, which is something that has become less fashionable in society generally in recent years. The emphasis has been on taking part rather than winning, where everyone is rewarded for their efforts, irrespective of their contribution to the result. But the fact is that you can't encourage high performance unless you are prepared to distinguish between those who are making a contribution and those who are not – and reward those who are performing well, while punishing those who are not.

That means that a leader needs to create a system where performance is measured – through a system that is understood by everyone – and rewarded. Again, the argument lies in basic human psychology. People like order, and they need to understand in a competitive environment such as the workplace who is being rewarded and who is not, and why. The difficulty for leaders in business is that it is not always clear, and this is particularly true of large companies, who is performing well and who is performing badly – indeed, sometimes it is only clear to the people immediately surrounding a poor performer that they are not producing good work, which can cause a great deal of resentment if their poor performance is not noticed by those higher up the organisation.

A good performance management system will allow people to see where they stand against others, and trust that everyone in the company has the same understanding. It gives certainty and it gives reassurance, as well as protecting the organisation from the more destructive trends in human behaviour. As the anthropologist Richard Dawkins argued, in the absence of solid evidence of a hierarchy, people will instead begin to rely on relationships for their survival. In other words, there are two ways of protecting yourself – to be strong, or to stand next to someone who is. If they cannot distinguish themselves based on their performance, people will spend their energy on identifying and developing relationships with others within the business that will make them feel safe, regardless of how they perform. This creates an organisation based on cliques and a 'bunker' mentality that can seriously harm collective performance.

SETTING THE TARGET

The first rule of effective performance management is that everyone needs to know exactly what is expected of them. If they don't, how can they possibly achieve it? In practice this means that the leader should set out a goal – the ultimate aim – and a clearly defined range of objectives that define that goal, from failure to achievement. And in order for the leader and the employee to assess whether they have achieved their objectives, there needs to be a system that assesses the individual's performance against the range of objectives, in a way that is easy to understand and transparent (meaning that if two or more people are asked whether the individual has achieved an objective, they will come up with the same answer). There is, in other words, no ambiguity about the result.

So let's start with the setting of the ultimate goal. As we discussed in Chapter 2, the best 'visions' (or objectives, or achievements), are what Andrew Meikle calls 'just about possible'. They are stretching and ambitious, but it is possible to imagine yourself achieving them. And there is a clear target, at which point you know that you have achieved the goal. Let's take a simple example, outside the field of business – the goal of climbing Everest. It's an ambitious objective, but one that many others have achieved, so is not unrealistic. The aim of undertaking the task is clear – it is to get to the top of the mountain (and, hopefully, down again in one piece). It's an easily understood objective, because climbers undertaking the challenge can see how far they've got to go, and know when they have reached the top (and achieved the objective). You either get there or you don't – achievement is not open to interpretation. And everyone will understand your achievement when you say you have climbed Everest – in other words, it is a meaningful objective.

A comparable objective in terms of business might be to land a major client. It's an objective that is also easy to understand as well as to measure, as the outcome will either be that the individual lands the client, or does not. Failure, incidentally, or at least the possibility of failure, is a vital ingredient in encouraging high performance. The risk that someone might fail, and fail publicly with all the humiliation that comes with that, is a great motivator.

But not every task has a black or white, yes or no, binary outcome. Life is generally more complicated than that. So it is more likely that the leader will be dealing with a task or objective where there are a range of possible outcomes, and will have to decide what level of performance is to be expected from each employee, and how that performance expectation can be communicated and measured.

In the business world, a range of outcomes may equate to, say, the performance in terms of revenue by members of a sales team. Some members of the team will naturally perform better than others and so in any team you will have a range of outcomes which are set by the best and worst performer. Generally, the smaller the range of possible outcomes, the greater the pressure on individuals to perform – the distinction between the best and the second best is enormous to the individual concerned, whereas in a large team of, say, 20 members, an individual is less likely to be concerned if they are ranked between 11 and 18 because the distinction is not so apparent.

Each member of the team can be 'marked' on their performance. Some members of the team may consistently perform at a rate of nine out of ten – in practice, this may mean that every year they exceed their sales target. Others may only just hit their target every year, or sometimes exceed it by a narrow margin. They are performing at a rate of seven or eight in the range. And a few will consistently miss their target – they may be considered to be fives out of ten.

But again, the business world is a complex one and gauging performance levels within a range of outcomes can be a real challenge. Performance cannot always be measured in terms of money brought in, clients won or sales made. Sometimes it has to be measured on a basis that is closer to, say, the judging of a gymnastics competition where judges score each competitor based on their technique, style and presentation. But whatever the performance measurement system is, what is important is that it is clearly understood by everyone, that it is trusted (in the sense that people believe that their performance will be assessed and marked accurately) and it must be believable. The best systems are simple ones based around a small number of measures, which are relevant to as many of the participants as possible.

THE ✓, X, ? TEST

Another way of looking at this is to write down the names of everyone on your team, and then next to each name write a tick, a cross or a question mark. The ticks go to everyone who meets or exceeds your expectations. A cross goes against anyone who has failed to meet your expectations consistently over the past six months or more (an occasional blip in performance should be allowed and even expected – it's only time to get worried when someone performs poorly consistently over a reasonable length of time). Finally, a question mark goes against anyone who you consider to be a variable or unpredictable performer, a developing performer who could improve or equally, get worse in the future and you're not sure which way they will go, or someone you don't know well enough yet to judge.

Any team will have a range of ticks, crosses and question marks. But that is not to say that you have a collection of excellent performers, a few duds and a couple of unknowns. What you have is a collection of people who all need your attention as a leader in order to improve or turn in consistently high performance, but each needs a different type of attention and different tactics in order to get the best from them.

An alternative way of looking at this is to plot every member of the team on a graph according to their competence and their commitment to the job:

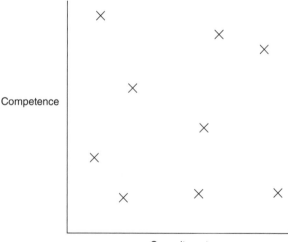

Where each team member stands on the grid tells the leader the best way of improving their performance:

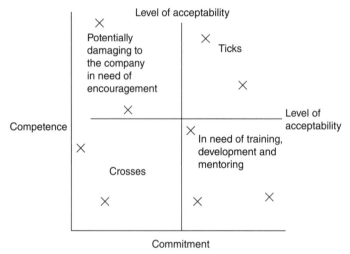

Source: Peter Chambers, Vistage International

GETTING THE BALANCE RIGHT

It's vital that the leader gets the performance balance right in a team. Too many fives out of ten on the team, and the better performers – the nines out of ten – can easily become disillusioned because however good their performance, the team result is always dragged down by the lower performers. There is also a danger that the best performers can become complacent and lazy, or even arrogant, if there are too many average performers on their team, because they are able to distinguish themselves as better performers without a great deal of effort. Conversely, if there are too many nines out of ten on a team it becomes difficult to stand out from the crowd for your high performance, which is discouraging – but generally, the better the worst performer on a team, the greater the pressure on the best to perform.

Getting the best from each will mean a combination of providing training to the people who can improve, 'punishment' (which is in inverted commas because we don't mean literally beating poor performers with a stick) and rewards. As we discussed in the motivation chapter and as the writer Daniel Pink has pointed out, providing an incentive to the best performers doesn't mean money, necessarily – although performance-related pay remains as popular as ever, in spite of conflicting evidence that it actually works effectively to encourage the best performance. Andrew Meikle argues that you need to offer performers something that brings them significant emotional pleasure in order for the incentive to work effectively. For some, this might mean money or the promise of promotion and career progression, but basic human nature means that it is far more likely that recognition – meaning public recognition as being a strong performer compared against others – is the most effective incentive in business. People should get what they deserve. There should be consequences for good performance but equally, consequences for poor performance.

DEALING WITH HIGH PERFORMERS

Let's start with the ticks, the nine and ten out of tens. The best performers need stretching targets so they can always improve, but above all they need recognition. Talented people should be treated differently; they are special and they have earned the right to be treated as such. If someone is good, they should be told so, and often.

The risk with high performers is that they can slip into complacency if they are not sufficiently challenged or stretched. An example of this was seen in a recruitment consultancy a few years ago. The star performer of the team was Clive, a senior recruitment consultant who had been consistently the highest earner in terms of fees over the previous few years. But his performance then began to slip. One year, he billed £650,000, easily the best performance in the organisation and the only consultant to bill over £500,000 in any year. The following year, he billed £540,000 – but was still easily the best performer on the team. His immediate boss, however, was becoming concerned that Clive was coasting and agonised over the best way to tackle the problem. Eventually, he called Clive into his office and asked him how he felt about his performance in the most recent financial year. 'Great,' said Clive, 'I'm number one again! The only consultant to earn over half a million.' And he gave the thumbs-up. So his boss told him to sit down and told him that, compared with his performance in the previous financial year, when he had billed £650,000 in fees, his performance this year had only been average. And, continued his boss, it would really depress him to see Clive accepting an average performance so if that was the way he was going to continue, perhaps he should leave.

Clive's reaction was fairly predictable for a successful salesman who was used to constant praise – he stormed out of the office and ignored his boss for the best part of two weeks. But then he came back and thanked his leader for giving him the shock he needed to re-energise his performance. The following year, Clive billed over £700,000 and demanded constantly high performance from his own team. That said, the leader's tactic was a risk, albeit a well-judged one, because the last thing he wanted was for Clive to leave the company. The point of this tale is that no two high-performers are the same and a leader can only work out the best way to manage them and to continually encourage them to perform well if they know each and every one, and understand what makes them tick (and what makes them walk out in a huff). There is no fail-safe method for dealing with high-performers, or with any member of the team – it's all about knowing your people as well as you can.

DEVELOPING PERFORMERS

Let's move on to the question marks, the fives out of ten – those members of the team who are not performing as well as you expect them to, or who are still developing as performers. The first step is to find out why they are not performing as well as you think they could, and if they are aware that they are. It's usually a good idea to gather feedback from other people in the organisation, to check that your assessment of their performance is reasonable. The next step is to sit down for a one-to-one meeting with the individual in question. This is a conversation that will need to be handled with care – you should both come out of it with a common understanding of what was said, and a clear plan to deal with any problems that have been raised.

It's tempting to begin by saying that you think that their performance is unsatisfactory but that's hardly a good start to a conversation if your aim (as it should be) is to find a way of transforming a question mark into a tick. So begin by asking them how they feel about their performance. The chances are that they already know that their work is not up to scratch and will feel relieved at the opportunity to tell you what they think the problem is. If, on the other hand, they genuinely seem to think that their performance is fine, you have a problem and they are already well on their way to becoming a cross.

The following discussion should form a clear plan to deal with any problems and form a path to help them improve their performance, marked with a series of clearly measurable and measured outcomes along the way, so progress can be monitored and understood by both of you. If the root of their underperformance is a hole in their knowledge or a lack of specific skills, it can usually be resolved through appropriate training. Developing performers need the most support but there should always be a clear plan with measurable outcomes. And while it's important to be optimistic about the outcome, you should always be clear about the consequences if their underperformance continues. If a leader wants to encourage high performance the message has to be that we will support developing performers, but will not tolerate poor performance.

DEALING WITH POOR PERFORMANCE

The crosses in your team, or those that show a consistent trend towards underperformance – meaning over the space of at least six months – are a more critical problem. There should be a clear dividing line between the question marks on your team – who you believe could and should improve – and the crosses, who have been given a chance but who have failed to reach expectations. Underperformers are never easy to tackle, which is why many leaders will tend to avoid the issue for as long as possible. In fact, most organisations are slow at addressing underperformers but those that are not tend to stand out from the crowd. Companies that set high standards get high performance.

While Jack Welch was chief executive of GE, for example, he was notorious for regularly sacking poorer performers. Everyone in the company was ranked according to their performance and every year, the lowest 10% were fired. It sounds terrifying (and no doubt was, if you were drifting near the culling line), but people still clamoured to be hired by GE, because the best people will always want to work with other good people. Brutal as Welch's regime sounds, he recognised the importance of taking action when employees failed to meet the expected standards of performance. The reality is that most people would rather work in a business that does not put up with sloppy work than in one that is prepared to tolerate it.

Some underperformers can improve with carefully targeted training and with the right support, and a leader should always make sure that they have done everything they can to help someone with potential develop. But inevitably, not all of the developing performers in a team will improve. For some, the problem may be a lack of motivation rather than a hole in their knowledge or set of skills, and that is more difficult to tackle as no amount of training will help them improve. Demotivated workers sap the energy of an organisation and it is the leader's task to do their best to transform them into someone who creates energy and motivates the people around them. But if the leader fails, their only option is to get rid of the worker, which should be done as humanely and generously as possible.

FIRING

It's inevitable that at some point in their career, a leader will have to fire someone. Or 'let them go' – however you choose to phrase it, it's not a pleasant experience for either party. Nevertheless, it is important that leaders deal with the task as well as they can, as their actions and behaviour will always have an impact on the employer brand (meaning its reputation as an employer, both inside and outside of the organisation). All employees, former and current, talk about their employer and the fact that someone has not performed well does not mean that they will not be popular with other workers, in your business and elsewhere. A bad 'reference' can do untold damage to the morale of existing employees and to the business' ability to recruit the best in the future.

The first point is to be fair, particularly when someone is being dismissed because of poor performance. A business with a good performance management system in place, one that is designed to encourage high performance, should have clear and measurable performance stand-ards in place, that are well understood by everyone. Everyone should have been given a clear explanation of the performance levels expected of them, and their per-formance should be regularly discussed, whether it is good or bad. They should also understand clearly the consequences of underperformance. The employee should be given clear reasons for the decision and an explanation of what will happen next; how long they will have to make alternative arrangements, whether they will be expected to work out their notice period, and any help or support that the company will offer them.

CREATING THE NEXT GENERATION OF LEADERS

As well as nurturing the team to coax the best possible performance from everyone, a leader should also be constantly on the lookout for the next generation of leaders. All organisations need continuity but leadership succession is often something that is neglected, even by some of the best-known and largest companies. In extreme cases the lack of an apparent successor to a well-known leader can be create a feeling of instability inside and outside the organisation. Take, for example, the ongoing speculation about the future of Apple. Its share price has fluctuated wildly in the past according to the state of health of its charismatic CEO, Steve Jobs, who has had a liver transplant. Jobs is seen as essential to the company's success, just as Bill Gates was to Microsoft. Gates' own succession was meticulously planned and took place between 2000 and 2006, when Gates steadily stepped away in stages from leadership responsibility.

It is possible that some of the nervousness around succession planning is down to the fact that current leaders are nervous about the process of identifying and developing a successor because they naturally see a potential threat, or the end of their days in charge. But developing future leaders is not a purely altruistic act – the fact is that often the biggest hurdle to a leader's own career progression is the lack of a competent number two. As people become more senior in an organisation it becomes more difficult to promote them or move them into a new role because that process creates a vacancy in their current position that may be difficult to fill. That is why anyone in a position of responsibility should always make sure that they have a reliable and talent deputy, who is identified clearly as a successor and who is well-prepared for the role. By making sure that there is someone available and with the ability and knowledge to step into their shoes, leaders improve their own prospects as well as that of their company.

WHO SAID IT

"Successful companies don't wait for leaders to come along. They actively seek out people with leadership potential and expose them to career experiences that are designed to develop that potential."
– **John Kotter**

A word of warning here; many leaders have made the mistake of choosing as their successor someone who is just like them, with similar values and beliefs, who will follow a similar strategic path and continue with their 'legacy'. This is invariably a mistake. Companies tend to thrive on change – and the ability to react to change is a vital necessity in the modern business world. Of course, preparing someone for your own job is not a particularly comfortable exercise, but leaders argue that having someone in their shadow who is keen and almost ready to step into their place helps to ensure that their own performance stays sharp.

WHO SAID IT

"I always hire people who absolutely want my job. Not just in a 'that would be nice to have her job' way but in an absolute 'I can do better than her' attitude."
– Rebekah Wade
(CEO News International)

Developing the next generation of leaders is an active rather than a passive exercise. This often means taking a risk, or at least a jump of faith, by giving people with potential a task or project that stretches them, and sitting back while they do it, even if they make mistakes. In fact, many experienced leaders say that trial and error (carried out within a supportive environment) is by far the most effective way for anyone to learn essential leadership skills.

WHO YOU NEED TO KNOW
– *Steve Jobs*

Jobs, who was born in San Francisco in 1955, founded Apple with three friends in 1976. The Macintosh, the first successful mass-market personal computer, was marketed about eight years later. Jobs left the company after a boardroom dispute in 1985 and set up NeXT, a computer platform development company, but rejoined Apple 11 years later when NeXT was bought by the group. During his time away from Apple he bought Lucasfilm's computer graphics business, which under its new name of Pixar produced classic children's films including *Toy Story* and *Monsters Inc.*

Jobs became interim CEO of Apple in 1998 and official CEO in 2000. Apple's development of new products such as the iPod, iPhone and iPad under his leadership have made the company one of the most famous in the world, although so synonymous has Jobs become with the success of Apple that its stock plunged when reports of his ill-health emerged. Jobs underwent a successful liver transplant in 2009.

Jobs is seen as a charismatic leader and an outstanding salesman, to the extent that the phrase 'the Steve Jobs effect' has entered business language to describe the state of fervour he instils in fans of Apple products. Jobs' philosophy for Apple, he has said, was to follow the advice of the Canadian ice hockey player Wayne Gretzky: 'Skate to where the puck is going to be, not where it has been.'

A HIGH PERFORMANCE ENVIRONMENT

There is more to high performance that simply dealing with the people involved. Leaders who want to encourage the best out of their people need to be sure not only that they hire and train the best, but that they create an environment in which high performance is not only possible, but encouraged. In practice, this means minimising the problems that are faced by the team, and maximising the support available to them.

As we have seen, people need the right information in order to deliver the best performance – meaning that they need to know exactly what is expected of them, the timelines they are expected to deliver within, and how their performance will be measured and assessed. But they also need the right tools to do the work, meaning the right technology and equipment, the right training, the right people in their team and a reliable communication. It is the role of the leader to make sure that all these are in place. And it's important to get the balance right – if people feel challenged but do not feel that they have enough support to do their job properly, they will feel stressed and burnt out. If they have plenty of support but are not sufficiently stretched and challenged, complacency can quickly set in. Without the right environment in which to work, even the best performer will soon deteriorate.

WHAT YOU NEED TO READ

▶ There are a number of good books available on performance, many of which also discuss effective team building. *How to Lead a Winning Team* by Morris, Willcocks and Knasel (Prentice Hall, 1995) is written from a leadership perspective and is particularly useful. *First Break All The Rules*, by fomer Gallup consultants Marcus Buckingham and Curt Coffman (Simon & Schuster, 1999) is a very readable and practical guide to encouraging high performance.

▶ Some valuable tips about high performance come from elite athletes and sportsmen – their disciplines may be very different from business, but the psychological techniques used by sportsmen during training and competition are widely recognised as having equal relevance in the workplace. Former athletes who now advise companies on high performance include Roger Black and Steve Backley (*www.backleyblack.com*)

▶ Graham Jones, a psychologist, and the former Olympic swimmer, Adrian Moorhouse, have

set up a performance consultancy (www
.lane4performance.com) that advises businesses on achieving high performance. Jones'
article 'How the best of the best get better and
better' in the *Harvard Business Review*, June
2008, pp 123–127 is an excellent summary of
some of their research into high performance. For more on Andrew Meikle's work on
high performance, see www.elkiem.com

IF YOU ONLY REMEMBER ONE THING

Recognition is the most powerful incentive
to performance.

CHAPTER 7

LEADING CHANGE

WHAT IT'S ALL ABOUT ➡

- ► Why change is necessary
- ► Why people are resistant to change
- ► How to communicate change
- ► The power of quick wins
- ► How to sustain change

No-one ever got anywhere by standing still. That is never truer than in the world of business. Any leader will have to deal with change at some point, whether they actively chose to or not, and for most it will be a real test of their leadership skills. The ability to foresee change, to deal with unexpected change, or to bring about fundamental change in an organisation is one of the most highly-regarded skills a leader can have – evidenced by the fact that some of the best-known business leaders in history have been those that have overseen transformation of the organisation they lead.

There is an argument that all businesses are operating in a constantly changing environment, but the concept of change can be broken down broadly into two main forms. There is the ongoing change that happens around a business – changes in technology, consumer demand, demographics and in the political and social landscape – that is effectively outside of its control. Nevertheless, the business must react to these changes if it is to survive. The pace of these changes has accelerated in recent years, thanks to advances in technology, to globalisation and deregulation, and the net effect is that no company can afford to stand still.

WHO SAID IT

"Doing what was done yesterday, or doing it 5% better, is no longer a formula for success. Major changes are more and more necessary to survive and compete."
– John Kotter

The second form of change is largely self-inflicted, but is usually a consequence of the first; the specific change initiatives that are introduced by the leader of a business in order to meet the demands of a new or changing environment, or to prepare the organisation better for the future. These changes might be planned – such as an acquisition, a wide-ranging marketing drive or a new corporate culture – or they could be sudden, in response to a crisis such as fraud or a PR disaster.

This is why you will frequently hear the argument (or a variation of it) that leadership is always about preparing an organisation for change. Anyone who has been a leader in business for any length of time, particularly during the past 30 years or so, will tell you that it's impossible to survive unless the business is prepared and flexible enough to cope with new developments as they occur. It's relatively rare that a leader is able to spot a change looming before it happens, but in many ways the most difficult task of all is for a leader to persuade people that change is necessary before it becomes apparent. If a business has already run into trouble, it's relatively easy to persuade people that it needs to change in order to improve. If everything is going well, there is little impetus for change at all – indeed, it's more difficult to persuade yourself and others that change is necessary because of the constant fear that you might make things worse at a time when everything seems to be going well.

CHANGE HAPPENS ANYWAY

A good example of companies anticipating or reacting to a change in consumer demand was seen a few years ago when there was a concerted drive towards healthy eating. Some of this was government-led but the most significant pressure came from a series of books, films and television programmes about the potential damage that high-fat foods could do, which included the film *Super-Size Me*, in which the filmmaker Morgan Spurlock spent a month eating nothing but food from McDonalds, the book *Fast Food Nation* by the investigative journalist Eric Scholsser, which looked at the wider impact on suppliers, farmers and society of America's addiction to junk food, and Jamie Oliver's television series about the poor nutritional content of many school lunches.

This all led to a hefty shift in demand by consumers, and to the expectations of society in general. Suddenly, everyone was talking about obesity and some of the staples of the fast food industry – burgers, chips, crisps and processed food in general – became a pariah. Obviously, this was going to have a serious impact on any business that was producing or selling food that was seen to fall into the 'junk' category. Arguably, the biggest fast food provider of them all, McDonalds, was relatively slow to react to the change – although once it did, it managed its campaign very successfully indeed. Others saw the change happening and realised they had to react, before things got worse.

Martin Glenn was, at the time, president of Walkers snack foods, which produced Walkers crisps. Glenn said he could see from an early stage the impact the debate was going to have on his business. The company knew that it was possible to blend their cooking oils with a version that had lower saturated fat, and that no-one would notice a difference in the taste, although it would be more expensive to produce its products as a result. 'So we decided to just go ahead and figure out how to pay for it later,' says Glenn. The company also switched its advertising emphasis to concentrate on the lower saturated fat and other lower calorie options, and took steps to actively engage in the debate over healthy eating. 'We had to, because we were in danger of being demonised over the issue,' says Glenn. 'How the business is seen in the wider world is absolutely critical.'

No change programme can happen without a leader and managing change will take an enormous amount of effort and time. Change has to come from the top and the leader has to be absolutely committed to it, and drive the process through right to its end. If the leader is not enthusiastic about the change he or she is advocating, there is no chance at all that anyone else will be.

THE RIGHT SORT OF CHANGE

It's part of a leader's role to constantly ask if an organisation is on the right track, and to anticipate changes that are happening to its market and business environment. It makes sense for a leader to regularly ask themselves four questions:

- ▶ What are the good things we do that we need to keep doing?
- ▶ What are the bad things we do that we need to stop doing?
- ▶ What are the things we do only occasionally, that we need to do consistently?
- ▶ What don't we do, that we need to start doing?

Of these four questions, the first and fourth are the most difficult. The first question is a potentially dangerous area because if things are going well it is very easy to become complacent. One school in London asks children, even if they have received 10 out of 10 for a piece of work, to ask themselves: 'www.ebi?' which means, 'What worked well: Even better if?' In other words, think about why it was good, and whether it could still be improved. It's a useful lesson for everyone.

The fourth question is difficult because it is by no means clear what the answer should be. This is what the former US Secretary of Defense Donald Rumsfeld might call the 'unknown unknowns' – it's difficult to know what you don't know. This is a particular challenge in business because companies tend to become inward-looking over time. One way of getting a different perspective of what a team or business does (and doesn't, but should do) is to ask a new recruit for their opinion – new joiners have, in effect, perfect vision because they have no experience of what has been done in the past.

If a major change is planned, it's important to be sure that it's the *right* change for the situation in hand. There's little point in change just for the sake of it – and it's not unusual for a leader to be faced with a situation where it's apparent that *something* needs to change, but it's not entirely clear *what*.

In other words, a leader must constantly ask questions, but must also be sure that they are the right questions. Let's go back to the shift in social opinion about healthy eating and junk food and the resulting change in demand from consumers that occurred in the US (and elsewhere) at around 2003. At about the same time one of the biggest companies in the world, McDonalds, was in the midst of its own crisis. It reported its first ever quarterly loss at the beginning of 2003 and it was clear that the company, and its brand, was in trouble. The change in social attitudes and the backlash against fast food was part of the problem, but an added concern for the company's management was that the term 'McJob' had just entered the *Oxford English Dictionary*. McDonalds had become synonymous with low-paid, menial, low-prospect jobs.

McDonalds underwent a near-miraculous transformation during 2003 and 2004, as worked to address the problems with its brand and reputation. In charge at the time were Jim Cantalupo, the company's CEO until his sudden death in April 2004, and Charlie Bell, its chief operating officer under Cantalupo, who took over as CEO after Cantalupo died. As part of the transformation process, the pair organised a series of workshops involving senior managers in the group, where they discussed what was going wrong and what could be done about it. One of these workshops was asked to look at the enormously high rate of staff turnover in the company. Charlie Bell walked into one of these sessions and asked the group what question they were trying to answer. He was told that they were discussing how to get employees to stay at McDonalds. Bell thought for a moment and told them that that was the wrong question; what they should be asking was, how can we make sure that young people leave McDonalds – better prepared for their future career?

What Bell did in that moment was turn a negative into a positive. The result was a radical investment by the company in training and development for staff at all levels, including a graduate track and a development programme for high potential employees. The company has since won a host of employer awards, including (in the UK) a Top 100 Graduate Employer award and a Britain's Top Employer award. In the space of a few years, the name of McDonalds has become an asset on someone's CV, rather than an object of ridicule.

WHO YOU NEED TO KNOW
Jim Cantalupo and Charlie Bell

Jim Cantalupo and Charlie Bell were two of the most influential leaders at the iconic US multinational McDonalds, although both had only a short reign as chief executive. Both men were long-time employees of the company, Bell first working behind a McDonalds counter at the age of 15 and Cantalupo, an accountant, joining the group as a financial controller in 1974 at the age of 30.

The pair is credited with turning around McDonalds when it hit a low point after years of over-expansion and a lack of innovation. Cantalupo, who had previously served as chairman of the organisation, came out of retirement in 2003 to take the post of CEO, with Bell as his chief operating officer, when the share price hit an all-time low of $13. They introduced the 'Plan to Win' programme, which overhauled the company's products and its marketing, as well as streamlining its operations and improving its service. Within six months, profits had increased by 25% and sales were at their highest level for 17 years.

The Australian Charlie Bell was the first non-American to lead the company and took over as CEO after Cantalupo's sudden death in April 2004 until he was forced to resign due to ill health in November 2004. He died in January 2005 at the age of 44. During his short time as CEO Bell led the initiative to introduce healthy options in McDonald's restaurants and to eliminate the 'supersize' option. At the time it was widely questioned whether Bell could ever successfully introduce such fundamental changes to an organisation that had been operating for so long in the same way, but the plan was so successful that it has become a case study in business schools worldwide.

WHY MOST CHANGE INITIATIVES FAIL

One of the most widely quoted statistics in business is that 75% of all change initiatives fail. It's not very encouraging, is it? The cause usually comes down to a lack of commitment – a company board, for example, spends weeks or months talking about the need for change, and then fails to carry this message and enthusiasm through to the rest of the organisation. Simply deciding that change is necessary is never enough – you have to make it happen. It's a huge task, and one that has to be undertaken with complete commitment by the leader.

The fundamental problem for a leader is that people are naturally resistant to change. This can be illustrated through a very simple experiment. Whatever you are doing, put the book down for a moment and fold your arms. You'll have done it without thinking, but for one reason or another (which might be connected to whether you are right or left handed but equally, might not), you will have folded your arms in the way you always do – left on top of right, or right on top of left. Now, unfold your arms and refold them in the opposite way – if you naturally fold them right on top of left, try the left on top of right. It doesn't feel right at all, does it? You need to think carefully about what you are doing – it's not an instinctive movement. If you fold your arms again in a few minutes without thinking about it, you will invariably revert to the way you always used to do it.

WHO SAID IT

"The difficulty is not developing new ideas, but escaping the old ones."
– John Maynard Keynes

The danger for a leader trying to instigate a change programme is that their followers will pay lip service to the idea, and then carry on as they always have. Leaders have to fight against this natural resistance to change, and that begins by providing a clear and compelling reason why the change is necessary. People need to understand what the objective is, whether it is a problem that needs to be addressed or an opportunity that should be grasped, as well as a rough time frame over which the change will occur. Often this means explaining how the change will benefit employees, or articulating an inspirational vision of the future that will emerge as a result of the change (US President Barack Obama's election campaign, 'Yes we can', was a classic example of the latter).

A FORMULA FOR CHANGE

The most influential writer and academic on the subject of change, leadership and business is John Kotter, professor at Harvard Business School. As part of his studies into change, and his work with many organisations around the world who have implemented change programmes, Kotter has identified a clear series of steps that will help a leader successfully introduce a change initiative.

This process begins with setting a vision, or a clear reason for the change and communicating it clearly and as often as possible. People need a good reason to change their way of doing things – they need to believe and understand the reasons for doing it, and they need to see the potential benefits to themselves as well as to the organisation as a whole. Another vital step, Kotter argues, is to establish a sense of urgency, which is crucial to creating the momentum and ignite the motivation that will carry a lengthy change process through to its conclusion.

There are a variety of ways in which a leader can do this, but the main ingredients is a hefty dose of honesty about what's happening with the company, what's happening to its market and what its competitors are already doing about it. They also need to be clear about the consequences if they do not change. As we discussed in Chapter 2, the identification of a common enemy can be very motivating to a group of people who need a sense of common purpose, so the threat of being overtaken by a competitor, or of the company been virtually destroyed if it fails to adapt to changing circumstances, often work as a motivating technique. A leader needs to get people thinking and talking about the need for change, and what is going to be done about it, before anything else happens. Without this foundation, the chances are that a change initiative will fail.

COMMUNICATING CHANGE

One of the most common reasons behind the failure of a change programme is poor communication – not so much that the programme is communicated poorly, but that it is not communicated frequently or forcefully enough. Often this is simply because a company's board or management underestimates how often the message will have to be repeated before it fully filters down through all levels of the organisation. There is always a danger that, by the time the message has been heard and understood by the last employee, management has already moved on to something else.

The first step for a leader is to make sure that the message is succinct and easily understood. As we have seen, in order for people to accept that change is necessary and to create the energy to achieve it, they need to understand the reasoning behind it. The challenge for the leader is to distil what may be a series of very complex reasons for change into a few sentences – this means identifying the core reason behind the need for change (which may be, for instance, adapting to changing consumer behaviour caused by the internet) and summarising it into a couple of short sentences or, even better, a sound bite. There will, of course, be a much longer standard speech around this message that the leader will repeat frequently, but the short, sharp explanation will form the core of the communications campaign.

Take, for example, the change programme introduced by Marks & Spencer a few years ago to address social concerns about sustainability and a potential backlash against large grocery retailers that might result. In reality, this meant addressing a wide range of complex issues, from concerns about excess packaging and plastic bags to the criticism that supermarkets were damaging local businesses and suppliers and encouraging mass production of food that was damaging the environment. The company's chief executive, Sir Stuart Rose, introduced a series of changes, which included reducing its packaging, removing additives from its food where possible and using sustainable sources where it could, and charging for plastic bags. But all of these changes were summed up in its 'vision' for change: 'Plan A – because there is no Plan B.' As motivational explanations go, it was perfect – simple, inspiring, urgent and easily understood.

Once a leader has found a simple and compelling reason for change, the next step is to repeat it until they think they can stand to hear it no more, and then repeat it again. There is no real shortcut to effective communication of change – you just have to repeat the same message, over and over again, until it becomes part of the fabric of the organisation. Remember that the message will have to compete with many others to be heard – employees and customers of most organisations these days are bombarded with daily communications on no end of subjects. So a message as important as this one needs some serious support behind it. It needs to be not only repeated and repeated, but reinforced by the behaviour of the leader, and the people around the leader. The management of a company simply has to be onside if a change programme has any chance of success at all – the management writer John Kotter argues that unless three-quarters of a company's management agree with and support the change, it will fail.

WHO YOU NEED TO KNOW
John Kotter

Born in 1947, the American business author and professor at Harvard Business School, is seen as the leading authority on change management and on the role of leadership in bringing about change. He became one of the youngest professors' in Harvard's history on his appointment at the age of 33. Kotter is a prolific author and at least a dozen of the 18 books

he has written so far in his career
have reach best-seller status.

Kotter's best-known work is *Leading Change*, which
began as an article in the *Harvard Business Review*.
The book, which followed soon afterwards, laid
out an eight-step process for successful business
transformation: establish a sense of urgency;
create a coalition of willing partners; develop a
vision for change; communication the vision;
empower employees to take action; generate
short-term wins; consolidate the gains; and anchor
the new approach in the culture of the business.
Throughout his work on change in organisations
Kotter has consistently said that leadership is the
engine that drives any change programme, and
that if the business has a purely managerial
mindset, the change initiative will invariably fail.

Kotter's other books include *What Leaders
Really Do* and *The Leadership Factor*, and his
articles appear regularly in the *Harvard Business
Review*. He recently set up Kotter International, a
leadership organisation aimed at helping leaders
develop the practical skills needed to lead
change in complex businesses.

CREATE A COALITION

An important step in making sure that the message is understood and accepted throughout an organisation is the 'recruitment' of supporters, both in terms of those that agree that the change is important and necessary, but also those that represent change by their very existence. John Kotter called this process a recruitment of a coalition of the willing. This is particularly important if the leader wants to change the culture of an organisation or group – if you have people in the team who will in themselves change the culture, simply through the way they behave or lead others, that is more than half of the battle. Ideally, these people should be drawn from all levels and departments of the organisation but should have two things in common – they should have influence over others (which does not necessarily have to come through the company hierarchy, but could come through specific skills or simply popularity), and they must be committed to the change programme. This team will help the leader spread the communication of change, and maintain the necessary momentum to see the change programme through to its conclusion.

Often the biggest difficulty faced by a leader instigating a change programme is making people believe that change was possible, particularly if it has been promised in the past but has not emerged. One of the most difficult challenges in persuading people that a change programme is necessary, and in keeping them onside, lies in managing their expectations about what can be achieved. People have a natural tendency to forget what has already been done and concentrate instead on the problems that have not yet been solved yet, as US President Barack Obama discovered over his first year of office. The expectations at his election were so high, mostly because his election campaign was so successful in persuading people that the US could be a better place, that the achievements he made, while considerable, never seemed quite good enough. Once again, the answer lies in constant communication, and reminding people of what you have already done as well of what you still intend to do.

THE IMPORTANCE OF QUICK WINS

The most effective way of persuading people that a change programme is working and that greater achievements are possible is to make sure that some results are almost immediately visible, even if the leader is manipulative in doing so. Nothing is more motivating than evidence of success. This might call on the need for a little manipulation by the leader, at least in terms of trumpeting successes that might otherwise go unnoticed. The key is to find a result, as early on in the change process as possible, that will allow people to see that the change programme is having an effect. Identifying and celebrating a series of small successes will help head of criticism of the change programme, or any negativity that is developing around it.

Any change programme should be accompanied by a carefully-developed strategy to make it happen. Ideally, this process should include a number of short-term targets that map the way to the end result. But if this is difficult to achieve, it would not hurt the leader at all to invent artificial targets and successes that show clearly that the change programme is working.

The leaders of significant change programmes say that 'quick wins' were absolutely vital in their ability to continue to push a difficult process of change through their organisation. These needn't be expensive or fundamental events, but they need to be visible, and relevant, to as many people as possible. And once the 'wins' are identified and completed, they should be publicly celebrated and the story of the win repeated as often as possible to as many people as possible, to show that results are not only achievable, but have been reached.

The first step is to find out what people within the organisation would change, if they had the chance. Heather Rabbatts, who was appointed as leader of the London Borough of Lambeth at a time when the Authority was in a deep financial and administrative crisis, achieved an impressive improvement in the organisation's budget and efficiency in the space of five years. With morale among employees at a desperate low, Rabbatts spent the first few months as leader visiting every office and location, as well as speaking to tenants and other users of the Authority's services, making sure that she spoke to people at all levels throughout the organisation to find out what they thought about how it was run, and what they would like to see changed.

One of the recurring complaints was that any repairs to council housing or other Authority-run sites, such as parks, took too long to arrange and as a result, many of the buildings were in a state of disrepair and employees were faced with constant criticism from local people. Rabbatts saw an ideal opportunity to deliver a quick and visible result, and so 'broke every procurement rule in the book' by insisting that every broken light bulb on every Authority-run estate in the borough was replaced. 60,000 bulbs were replaced over the following few weeks – an exercise that was expensive, but invaluable for the goodwill it created. The strategy bought the Authority the time it needed to correct the more complicated problem around its housing repairs processes. 'You have to have visible changes that people can get hold of, particularly when you are running an organisation that deals with the stuff of life,' is how Rabbatts explains her plan. 'People are not interested in fancy strategies; they want lights that work. If you put enough of those in place, you win some credit to get some of the longer-term changes through.'

Greg Dyke ran a similar strategy at the BBC and during his first few months as director-general and corrected as many of the complaints that he had heard from staff as he could, however small they were.

The most visible 'win' for Dyke, though, was the refurbishment of the BBC's offices in White City in London. The building was a standard, uninspiring 1970s design but its one attractive feature was an atrium at the centre, which no-one was allowed into on health and safety grounds. After a bit of investigation, Dyke was told that the problem was that the atrium did not have enough exits in case of an emergency, and there was no ramp for wheelchairs. He immediately saw the opportunity to do something that would impact hundreds of his staff, and spent around £100,000 to make the changes that were needed and opened the atrium up to all BBC employees, adding barbeques and a bar in the summer and throwing a party on the opening night. The White City building became symbolic of the change he planned to bring to the organisation – it told the employees that things could be changed.

SUSTAIN THE CHANGE

John Kotter argues that many change programmes fail because victory is declared too early, when people think the process is over and stop working at it. Quick wins are vital in keeping motivation and momentum going, but the focus should always be on the ultimate goal – and that goal is not always static. Kotter believes that long-term change requires the constant re-evaluation of the end target, and that the leader should always look for further ways of changing and improving the company. In practice, this means assessing the impact of each success-fully met target, analysing what went right and asking yourself if anything could be done any better. Kotter adds the warning that 'in reality, change programmes are messy and full of surprises', which is why it is essential that the leader must have a clear vision of where the organisation is ultimately heading, even if it does not get there exactly as planned.

The sign of a successful change programme is that, ulti-mately, the change stops being a process and becomes a core part of the business, part of its very culture. This means that where people used to do things instinctively in one way, the change programme means that now, they instinctively do it in the new way. It means that the leaders of the change programme throughout the organisation are replaced as they move on, to make sure that the values they represent are sustained. And it means that the change becomes part of the values and ideals imparted to new recruits.

When people talk about changing an organisation you will often hear the phrase 'turning around a juggernaut' (or a variation of it) crop up. This is an indication of what a challenge change can be, particularly in a large and established company. Change is not easy to bring about, but it is possible with the right level of commitment from the leader. Warren Buffet, the investment guru, once interviewed McDonalds' chief executive Charlie Bell about the company's change programme 'Plan to Win' and made the comment that transforming a group as large as McDonalds was like trying to turn around an oil tanker. 'I don't see us as an oil tanker,' replied, Bell, 'I see us as a fleet of speedboats.' Bell and his predecessor managed to transform McDonalds' fortunes in less than two years – given the size of the group and the fundamental change to the company culture that was required, it must be a lesson that anything is possible.

Change is one of the most difficult things for a leader to bring about in a business but it is also something that absolutely must be owned entirely by the leader. The good news is that there is a well-recognised process to successfully introducing a change programme, which has been identified by the many academic studies of change, and most significantly the work of John Kotter. Change begins with the vision of the leader, and a clear explanation of why it is needed. It is propelled by a sense of urgency that is created by the leader , through the recruitment of supporters within the organisation at all levels who help to keep the momentum moving, and through the enthusiasm that is generated by visible achievements along the way. And it is only finished when the change becomes part of the everyday life of the business.

WHAT YOU NEED TO READ

▶ John Kotter's book *Leading Change* (Harvard Business School Press, 1996) is essential reading, simply because it is seen as the 'bible' on change leadership. Kotter's website (www .kotterinternational.com), is another useful source of information about change management and other aspects of leadership.

▶ *Champions of Change* by David Nadler (Jossey Bass, 1998) is published in the US but, if you can find it, is a good summary of the challenges of change management. And *Leading Change Management* by David Herold and Donald Fedor (Kogan Page, 2008) is based on the authors' studies of change at 300 companies.

▶ To learn lessons from a master in communication about how to inspire the possibility of change among your followers, read through any of Barack Obama's speeches during his election campaign (and subsequently). Most of them can be found at www.obamaspeeches .com.

IF YOU ONLY REMEMBER ONE THING

A change programme needs momentum, which can only be created by the leader. The leader must create a compelling reason for change and repeat the message constantly and consistently, until everyone in the organisation hears and understands.

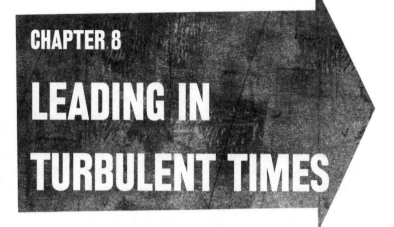

CHAPTER 8

LEADING IN TURBULENT TIMES

WHAT IT'S ALL ABOUT ➡

- ▶ How to lead through a crisis
- ▶ Ways of making decisions under pressure
- ▶ The importance of learning from experience
- ▶ Why you need to take risks
- ▶ Why you have to look after yourself

When times are tough, whether that's in business, in politics, in war or in life, people look for leaders to guide them through the storm. It's also true to say that a crisis will quickly sort out good leaders from bad – and sometimes result in the end of a good leader simply because people need to see evidence of change. This has been seen time and time again during the financial crisis and recession of 2008 and 2009 – numerous businesses and companies brought in new leaders, sometimes to address specific problems and sometimes just to show everyone that 'something was being done'. On the largest scale, the US looked for a new President during one of the most strife-ridden times of its recent history. It's interesting that the leader they turned to was the one who offered the greatest hope, and a clear promise that the American people were capable of seeing through the crisis and creating a better life for themselves.

The difference between management and leadership is most clearly highlighted in times of crisis. Whether a business is affected by an internal mistake, or whether it is impacted by a crisis in the environment or market in which it operates (such as a recession), it needs a leader to take charge, rather than a manager. Managers tend to address any problems by choosing the right course of action from an established selection of processes and procedures – in other words, they know through experience that things can be done and problems solved by following a plan that has been predetermined and has worked in the past. Leaders, on the other hand, tend to look for original solutions to problems. Rather than follow a fixed course, they set a clear direction, prepare the business for the change and work on translating anxiety into confidence.

This is the essence of why people look for leaders rather than managers during times of crisis. The best laid plans can be spectacularly disrupted by economic or political events, and for that reason the manager's route of following systems and processes can quickly become unreliable during a time of crisis. Instead, people look for a leader who will identify a clear path through the turmoil and make them feel that their worst fears can be overcome.

LEADING THROUGH A CRISIS

Crises may come in different forms, with varying degrees of danger to the business. Some may be internal and pass unnoticed outside of the organisation, while creating havoc within. Others are more public and wide-ranging. There are the enormous, survival-threatening disasters, of which the oil leak suffered by BP in the Gulf in Mexico is a recent and extreme example. There are crises that impact an entire industry, and which can affect any business in that sector, fairly or unfairly – such as the impact of the credit crunch on banks. There are economic crises, such as a recession, that affect all businesses but some more than others. And there are company-specific disasters, from fraud to fire or even a bad business decision.

Whatever its form, a crisis creates specific problems that have to be addressed by the leader. One of the most serious consequences is inevitably the impact on the people in an organisation. During any crisis, people quickly become confused, disorientated, anxious and often illogical. They look for guidance and that must be provided by a strong and calm voice from the top which, above all, provides emotional reassurance that everything is being done to resolve the problem.

WHO YOU NEED TO KNOW
Sir Winston Churchill

Widely acknowledged as one of the greatest ever wartime leaders, Sir Winston Churchill was Prime Minister between 1940 and 1945, and again between 1951 and 1955. Born into the English aristocracy at Blenheim Palace in 1874, he entered Parliament at the age of 26, switching his allegiance from the Conservatives to the Liberal Party four years later (he would return to the

Conservatives in 1924). As First Lord of the Admiralty, he was instrumental in building Britain's naval strength in response to the dramatic expansion of Germany's forces in the run-up to the First World War. His previous career as a solider led him in 1916 to resign from the Cabinet to fight for six months on the Western Front.

Opinions about Churchill's skills as a leader vary, with some dwelling on the strategic mistakes he made during his time as Prime Minister. General Sir Alan Brooke, his military chief of staff, once wrote that Churchill 'had 10 ideas every day, only one of which was good, and he did not know which it was'. Others argue that his willingness to risks in engaging the enemy was the crucial difference in winning the Second World War. Churchill's main strength as a leader, though, was in his ability to inspire and to raise the country's morale during the darkest hours. His powers of oratory have become legendary.

THE EYE OF THE STORM

The way in which leaders behave after a catastrophic event illustrate the importance of providing emotional reassurance first and foremost – it may be on an exponentially larger scale than anything that many leaders will have to deal with, but the fundamental lessons remain the same. There is a reason, for instance, why New York mayor Rudy Giuliani is praised for his leadership in the immediate aftermath of the attacks on the World Trade Centre on 11 September 2001, while the behaviour of President George W. Bush was ridiculed. Giuliani was immediately visible in the hours after the towers collapsed, appearing almost constantly on television, close to the site, and providing calm reassurance that the authorities were working as hard as they could. He passed on any information he had as soon as possible, once he was sure that it was accurate. The reality was that few people knew what was really happening and events were beyond the control of any of the emergency services, military or politicians, but even so, Giuliani's regular appearances offered some level of reassurance that someone was in control at a time when New Yorkers, and the rest of the country, were desperate for it. George Bush, by contrast, was invisible in the hours immediately after the attack – for reasons that could be interpreted as understandable, since the Secret Service had no idea of whether more attacks were planned, and so took the necessary steps to protect the President by keeping him on board Air Force One and out of sight.

The other lesson here is that a crisis can make or break a leader. A crisis tends to erode trust in leaders, whether they have contributed to it or not. This is why 'honour' or integrity become particularly important leadership characteristics during a crisis. In order to maintain (or re-establish) trust in their leader, employees need to believe that the leader is remaining true to the beliefs that they have previously set out and are acting in the best interests of the company and its employees. In practice, a number of things will help to build that belief, such as transparency and honesty of communication, general competence in terms of skills, and remaining as visible as possible to employees.

In business, things rarely go to plan and it's inevitable that a leader will have to face a crisis at some point in their career. Those leaders that have lived through crises of their own, as well as leadership academics who have studied leaders in crisis, agree that there are clear steps and behaviour that a leader must follow in order to minimise any damage and maximise the chances of the organisation weathering the storm.

ACKNOWLEDGE THE CRISIS

The first step in successfully leading an organisation through a crisis is to acknowledge what is happening, and explain the problem and what you intend to do about it to your followers, as well as setting out exactly what is expected of them. In a difficult environment, it is human nature to look for certainty and order, as that helps people to feel as though they are in control of a situation that may seem uncontrollable. Denying a situation that may seem obvious to everyone, and which may be attracting comment from outside the business, is not going to help the situation – and yet denying that there is a problem is often the instinctive reaction of management.

This instinct to deny comes from an understandable desire to protect the business and its reputation, as well as the reputation of the leader. The phenomenon could be seen clearly in the aftermath of the oil spill in the Gulf of Mexico in 2010, following the explosion on BP's Deepwater Horizon rig. BP's leadership said repeatedly in public that the oil was dispersing, and initially underestimated the amount of oil that was spilling into the Gulf. The net effect was that, even when the statements that BP made were true, they were treated with scepticism and contempt by the media. Downplaying the extent of a problem serves only to create mistrust, among both employees and those outside the business. One the truth comes out – and it inevitably will – the automatic assumption will be either that the leader will lie about other things as well as the crisis itself, or that the leadership is incompetent because it did not know what was really going on. Neither is particularly helpful to the long-term health of a business.

In acknowledging a home-grown mistake a leader is also tacitly accepting ultimate responsibility, which is another important building block to the recovery of the business. If a leader is invisible during a crisis, the organisation will be seen as rudderless. Lee Iacocca, who as chief executive of Chrysler oversaw the turnaround of the US car manufacturer during the 1980s, has talked frequently of the importance of accountability in leadership. Iacocca took over as CEO of the struggling company at a time when it was near collapse, and introduced a drastic programme of cost-cutting and restructuring. He lobbied the US Congress to guarantee massive loans that would allow the company to stay in business during the restructuring and backed up his campaign with a series of press adverts which asked 'Would America be better off without Chrysler?' Each was signed by Iacocca, with the intention, he said, of sending the message that there was genuine accountability at Chrysler. 'A chief executive of a company that's going broke has to reassure people,' said Iocacco. 'He has to say, "I'm here, I'm real, and I'm responsible for this company. And to show that I mean it, I'm signing on the dotted line."'

Richard Branson is another leader who understands the power of an apology. Customers of Virgin Airways, who were delayed by 14 hours in Hong Kong when their flight to London was pulled off the runway because of a computer problem, were amazed to receive a phone call from Branson a few days later, apologising for the inconvenience. A group of people who had previously been annoyed with the airline, and who might have told others the story of their mammoth delay, instead began telling the story of how the chief executive of Virgin rang them personally to apologise.

WHO SAID IT

"Communication has to start with telling the truth, even when it's painful."
– Lee Iacocca, former CEO, Chrysler

TAKE DECISIVE AND QUICK ACTION

The ability to make good decisions most of the time is at the core of an effective leader. Making good decisions under pressure, though, is exceptionally difficult, particularly in the world of business where there are rarely rights and wrongs, only decisions that have consequences. It was once said that excellence in business was about being 80% right, because it deals with the uncertainty and unpredictability of human behaviour.

Most leaders take a very scientific attitude to decision-making and say they like to sit back and weigh up the risks before coming to a conclusion. Many are not afraid to admit that they often try to delay making a decision that they are under pressure to make on the basis that time often provides more information that will help them to make a better decision than they would have had they made it quickly. Some leaders (and, at the risk of generalisation, these tend to be male) see any delay in making a decision as a sign of weakness while others (and again, generalising, female leaders are more adept at this) actively seek to gather the views of others during the decision-making process. There is no right or wrong answer – every leader is different. But at times of crisis, quick action often makes the difference between success and failure.

No leader, particularly in a time of crisis or uncertainty, can afford to be vague. People need certainty and a feeling that someone is in charge, which means that a leader needs to set out what he or she plans to do, as quickly as possible and, unless the subsequent evidence suggests otherwise, stick firmly to their course. This often calls for a degree of courage, since any decision made during a crisis is likely to be a tough one.

Many leaders trust their instincts at times of crisis but if it's at all possible, a more thorough review of the situation and possible solutions is usually advisable. Military leaders are intensively trained in 'mission analysis' – the process of exhaustively analysing any particular task or mission which takes into account the capabilities of the leader's unit (in terms of man power, equipment and so

on), the constraints and restrictions (weather, the conditions of the location, etc), outside influences and the
strengths, weaknesses, intentions and capabilities of the
opponent. It is a thorough, formal and logical exercise
that is intended to eliminate as much of the risk as possible from decision-making. Military leaders who have
gone through the process frequently say that the end
result is that, eventually, they are able to make non-
intuitive decisions very quickly because they know what
questions to ask themselves.

Business leaders are rarely so intensively trained in the
decision-making process, which is why many are content
to trust their own instincts. But it stands to reason that
any decision would benefit from a close analysis of the
essentials of the situation, of the constraints and opportunities that are present, even if there is relatively little
time available in which to think. Often the problem in
business is that leaders are faced with too much information, which can cloud or paralyse their judgement, in
which case many leaders who have experienced a crisis
say they have no choice but to set a cut-off point at which
they decide to take on no further information, and just
make a decision.

COMMUNICATE

The second lesson for leaders is to communicate as often
and as honestly as possible with their people, and with

their customers. As we've already discussed, in the absence of solid information, people will tend to fill the vacuum with speculation and gossip – and that happens remarkably quickly thanks to the phenomenon of social media. If they say nothing to their people, leaders are still communicating with them – and not in a positive way. They are telling them that they are not important.

Leaders cannot solve any problem alone – they need the support, buy-in and commitment of their followers. And if people are going to accept the sometimes painful measures that will be necessary to deal with a crisis, they need to understand exactly why they are required. The ability to persuade others to follow you becomes much more critical in times of crisis than it does in the ordinary and everyday life of a business, because the stakes are much higher and people will be much more difficult to convince.

This means that the leader must reinforce the bond of mutual trust between them and their followers, and honest, open and frequent communication will form the foundation of that bond. It's vitally important that people know exactly what is going on, and what the leader plans to do about it, and that they learn this information first-hand and not from any outside source. It's usually better to get all of the bad news out of the way in one go, rather than be tempted to try to lessen the blow by releasing bits and pieces at a time – sometimes referred to as the 'salami' approach to communication. Releasing news over stages will only create anxiety that worse is to come.

Employees should also be given ample opportunity to ask questions and participate in a two-way dialogue. The more open and honest a leader is about a problem, the more trusted and engaged employees feel, and the more likely it is that they will put all of their efforts into working through the crisis.

It's inevitable in business that some crises cannot be addressed without making some employees redundant. Difficult as the situation may be, the same rules of communication apply. Those who are going to be asked to leave need to know first, and they should be told humanely. It's important in this case to focus communication on those who will be directly affected by the decision, and to do it before rumours have a chance to start. Perhaps the worst thing a leader can do when dealing with redundancy is to announce to the organisation as a whole that 15% of the workforce will have to lose their jobs, before deciding who will go – that does nothing but damage the morale of the entire organisation and foster an atmosphere of fear, resentment and mistrust. It's important to explain clearly the reasons behind the redundancies, and to reassure everyone that those who will have to leave will be given as much support as possible – both financial and in terms of helping them to find new employment.

Leaders who have seen through large-scale redundancies in an organisation say that treating those who will leave with dignity and as much generosity as possible is essential, both as a basic requirement of humanity but also in order to protect the morale of the organisation. Workers who remain with the organisation, and their performance, will inevitably be affected by the redundancies, and if they see that the people who have left have been treated and supported as well as possible, it is more likely that they will think more highly of the company and people they work for.

WHO YOU NEED TO KNOW
Lee Iacocca

Lida Iocacco (known as Lee) is one of the best-known American business leaders, renowned and widely studied for his time as CEO of the US car giant Chrysler Corporation in the 1980s. Iocacca studied at Princetown University before joining the Ford Motor Company in 1946, initially as an engineer but later in sales and marketing. He rose quickly through the ranks, becoming president of the company between 1970 and 1978 but argued with, and was fired by, Henry Ford II.

He was asked to join Chrysler soon afterwards, at a time when the group was close to collapse. He sold off the company's European operations to Peugeot and made large-scale redundancies. A loan guarantee from the US Congress enabled the company to remain afloat as it slowly recovered. Iocacco oversaw the development of new, smaller, less expensive car and van models that proved extremely popular with consumers. Throughout the 1980s Iocacca fronted Chrysler's advertising campaigns, two of which – 'The pride is back' and 'If you can find a better car, buy it' – have become inextricably linked with his name.

Iocacca retired from Chrysler in 1992. His books include *Where Have All the Leaders Gone?* which berates the quality of political leadership in the US and sets out the qualities that Iocacca believes all good leaders should have – curiosity, creativity, competence, charisma, courage, conviction and common sense.

DEALING WITH THE MEDIA

The question of how much to communicate outside of the business can be a tricky issue for leaders, and one that has become considerably more challenging thanks to the instantaneous world of social media and electronic communication. The internet, 24-hour rolling news, Twitter and Facebook have all made business everyone's business. Potential PR crises can come from anywhere – from a comment made by an employee or customer to a video on YouTube.

The temptation in a world of instant communication, particularly when you are under pressure to respond, is to react as quickly as possible to any crisis that becomes public. But that is not always the best course of action. Social media may be instantaneous but it is also lasting and far-reaching – if a leader makes a mistake or an unfortunate slip, it will be available for just about every-one to see or read.

DEALING WITH A PR CRISIS

If a leader is ever faced with a potential PR crisis, with luck there will be a PR expert somewhere in the wings to offer advice. Even so, there are a few hard and fast rules to follow when dealing with the media during a crisis:

► Stop to think before saying anything. The pressure to react quickly can be enormous, but it's not always the case that a response is necessary. Some things are quickly forgotten.

► Be as honest as possible. The truth will generally out and when it does and the leader has been seen to be less than honest, the damage to their credibility will be huge.

► Be calm and composed at all times. People need to know that the leader is in control of the situation.

► Consult. It's easy to lose perspective as a leader at the best of times but during a crisis, it's easy to become blinkered. An alternative perspective will help.

► Accept the blame, but share the credit. As a leader you must accept that you are ultimately responsible, even if you are not.

► Show that you have learned from the experience. People are generally more willing to forgive a transgression if it's apparent that lessons have been learned.

CRISIS MANAGEMENT IN PRACTICE

Let's look at a couple of real-life examples. A case study that is frequently used in leadership studies to illustrate how good communication can help to limit a potentially damaging situation is the 'syringe in a can' experience

of Pepsi in the mid-1990s. The story began with an isolated report on a local television station in Washington
State that a pensioner had found a syringe in a recently-
purchased can of Pepsi. Over the following six days, eight
more people appeared on local media outlets saying that
they had also found a syringe or needle in Pepsi cans and
on the same day, the report appeared on two national
news networks.

Pepsi's leaders knew that the story could soon get out of
control and cause severe damage to the brand and the
business. Their response was to stress from the outset that
the findings were nothing more than a series of hoaxes. As
part of the concerted media campaign waged by Pepsi to
protect itself, it said that it had to repeat its central message
– that the cans were safe – 'in 50 different ways'. The
company urged shop owners not to remove the cans from
their shelves while the findings were investigated and
released videos to the media showing how their cans were
manufactured and stressing that tampering with them in
its factories was impossible. When the police made an
arrest in connection with one of the incidents, Pepsi
insisted that the arrest be made public, and highlighted
the possible charges and penalties that could be brought.
The company also published full-page newspaper adverts
in which it said it was 'pleased to announce ... nothing'.

Within a month, the media was reporting the story as a
series of unrelated criminal acts and Pepsi brought out
a further advertising campaign celebrating its win over
potential sabotage and thanking the American people
for its support.

A negative press campaign against a business will inevitably have an impact on the morale of employees, and so often leaders are faced with a fight on two sides, seeing that outside communications are handled properly, while making sure that employees are fully informed and reassured and always hear critical information first, rather than from the media. Another leader who has had first-hand experience of a problem that threatened to become a PR disaster is Charles Dunstone, chief executive of the Carphone Warehouse. In April 2006 its Talk Talk division offered a free broadband to anyone who subscribed to its landline service. In the first few months over half a million people registered for the offer and it quickly became clear that the company could not cope with the demand. The customer service system buckled under the strain and customers were left waiting weeks and sometimes months for the service to be connected. To add to Dunstone's misery, the story generated enormous interest – and acres of negative coverage – in the press and broadcast media.

Dunstone has described the challenges of dealing with the crisis, both internally and externally. His employees were frazzled by the annoyance of their customers and the demands of the workload, and dejected by the intensely negative media coverage. One of the first things that Dunstone did was to write an email to everyone in the company, admitting that the mistake had been his, as well as outlining what he planned to do to address the situation. He signed the email 'from the idiot who thought of free broadband'.

Dunstone also made the decision to be as open as possible about the problems not only with his customers and employees, but with the press. He agrees with the argument that companies that honestly and openly admit their mistakes are more likely to ride out the media storm, but makes the point that, in Talk Talk's case, it also meant that the company 'became the media's whipping boy' for all broadband or communications problems. 'We were brutally honest about what was happening, but as we learned more about the situation we realised that we weren't in much more of a mess than many of our competitors, but they were keeping their heads below the parapet,' he says. He adds that, with hindsight, it's impossible to say whether being frank with the media was the right decision, although 'it was certainly the right choice internally and with our customers'.

LEARN FROM THE EXPERIENCE

WHO SAID IT

"The problem (in America today) is not that we fail, it is that we don't risk failing enough."
– Phil Knight (CEO Nike)

It's often said that we should all learn from our mistakes and business leaders are no exception. Mistakes are an inevitable part of life but the only way to turn a negative situation into a potentially positive one is to see a mistake as a learning exercise – thoroughly examine what went wrong, and see what you can do to minimise the chances of it ever happening again.

Talk Talk undoubtedly learned from its experiences. Dunstone says that the broadband disaster changed the entire thinking of the company, because it brought home the fact that it was now operating on a large scale and any mistakes would be far harder to fix. When the company was first set up its stock distribution system, which sent goods out to its stores, stopped working but its employees got all of its orders out on time simply by turning up at the warehouse, packing the goods themselves and sending them by post overnight. But a problem like the broadband offer could not be corrected so easily and from that point onwards, the company was far more careful and mature in the decisions it took.

Eric Schmidt, the chief executive of Google, argues that a level of arrogance is a basic requirement of leadership, because leaders of innovative companies have to believe that they can change the world, otherwise they would not try. But the reality is that no-one is perfect and so mistakes are inevitable, particularly when it comes to innovations such as Google. Schmidt says the company as a whole spends a lot of time talking about and learning from the mistakes it has made in the past.

All business involves risk and in a healthy organisation – meaning one where the leader has selected the best people possible and has given them the resources they need to get on with their job without interference – mistakes will invariably happen. But apportioning blame or punishment will inevitably affect the willingness of people to take risks, and innovate, in the future.

LOOKING AFTER YOURSELF

A crisis can be emotionally and physically exhausting for a leader, adding sometimes unbearable strain to a role that, even at the best of times, is highly pressurised. Leadership can be a lonely and demanding role, which is why many who have reached the top of their profession strongly advocate the need for leaders to create space for themselves to think and reflect. Many say that the pressure of leading a business means that, unless they actively create space and time for themselves, the quality of their decision-making and ability to innovate can suffer over time. In other words, leaders need to take time out to work *on* the business, looking ahead to anticipate future changes and opportunities, rather than *in* the business. 'One of the dangers of leadership roles is that the job can grind you down,' is how Greg Dyke puts it. 'You don't have enough time to find good new ideas.'

Experienced leaders emphasise the importance of taking 'time out' to recharge and to create space and perspective, which allows them to make better decisions. The primary role of a leader is, after all, to make good decisions, which means that they must do everything to preserve their ability to do so. Again, every leader is different in this respect – the former Prime Minister Margaret Thatcher was notorious for functioning on only three or four hours of sleep a night, and seemed to thrive on the pressure. The wartime leader Field Marshall Montgomery, on the other hand, would insist on eight hours' sleep in comfort whenever possible, on the basis that his brain had to function at its best if he was going to save peoples' lives.

Even the busiest of business leaders take time out to do something different, whether it's a sport or a hobby, or even spending time with their family, because it allows them to reset their perspective. The best leaders are also constantly learning, from their peers, mentors, from their mistakes, or from more formal sources such as leadership books. The academic and writer John Kotter once wrote that the element that sets a leader apart, particularly in the modern business world hat is charac-terised by dynamic, adaptive organisations and markets, is their ability to continuously learn and develop. These leaders show an ability to assess both their failures and their successes, are open to taking risks and trying new ideas, and are natural observers of people and go out of their way to seek opinions and find new ideas. Very few people could claim to be born leaders. Most become leaders by learning from experience and from the people around them.

Above all, good leaders care – about their organisation, about their people and about what they are all trying to achieve. They have a passion for what they do that can't be counterfeited and which they use to persuade the people around them of the worthiness of their cause. Leadership is a challenging, demanding and often lonely position but, done well, leaves a lasting legacy.

WHAT YOU NEED TO READ

▶ *Crisis Management: Master the Skills to Prevent Disasters* by Richard Luecke (Harvard Business School Press, 2004) is part of the 'Essentials' business series from Harvard Business School and contains no end of tips for coping with a huge variety of corporate crises. *New Strategies for Reputational Management* (Kogan Page, 2007) is written by a corporate communications expert, Andrew Griffin, and explains clearly how businesses can help to protect their reputation.

▶ Sometimes it's helpful to learn from the mistakes or others rather than to wait for your own. Jamie Oliver and Tony Goodwin's book

How They Blew It (Kogan Page, 2010) is a very entertaining account of some of the best-known business mistakes in recent times.

▶ Outside the world of business, it's difficult to find a more inspiring, or harrowing, account of leadership under pressure than the story of Nando Parrado, who was one of a team of young Uruguayan rugby players whose airplane crashed high in the Andes in 1972. Nando's book, *Miracle in the Andes*, was made into a film, *Alive*, and Nando is now a well-known motivational speaker (www.parrado .com).

IF YOU ONLY REMEMBER ONE THING

The best leaders learn from their mistakes and from their successes. Risk is a fact of life in business and companies cannot thrive without occasionally stepping into the unknown, or falling at a hurdle.

CONCLUSION

As we said at the outset, this book is intended to help you bring out the leader in you, and not to tell you how a 'typical' leader acts and behaves. There is no such thing as a typical leader. There are just people who know how to lead.

Good leaders can achieve amazing things. During difficult times – and there have been plenty of those in recent years – we look for people we can trust, who can lead us into a better future. Leadership means different things to different people, which is why many of us struggle to explain what makes a good leader. But what we all know, mostly from our own experiences of being led by others, is what a good leader makes us *feel*, about ourselves and about what we believe we can do. The best leaders make us feel that, with their help, we can achieve what we set out to do. They make us believe that anything is possible. That's why it's important to ask yourself from time to time: what does it feel like, to be led by me?

The best leaders are not leaders because they are ambitious; they are leaders because they have an idea or a plan that they passionately believe is worth following, and want to take others on their quest. They genuinely want to bring out the best in their people. A good leader can change someone's life for the better, can inspire them to great things and will leaving a lasting impression on the people around them. Isn't that who you want to be?

INDEX

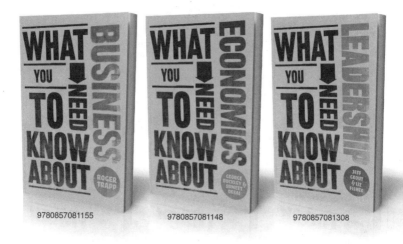
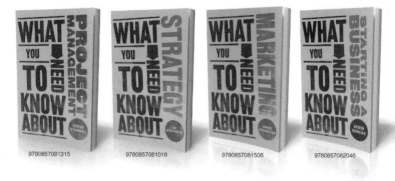